Mindy Ferguson

hugs Bible Reflections for Women

HOWARD BOOKS
A DIVISION OF SIMON & SCHUSTER
New York London Toronto Sydney

52 Inspirational Studies and Stories to Draw You Closer to God

Our purpose at Howard Books is to:

- Increase faith in the hearts of growing Christians
- Inspire holiness in the lives of believers
- Instill hope in the hearts of struggling people everywhere

Because He's coming again!

Published by Howard Books, a division of Simon & Schuster, Inc.
1230 Avenue of the Americas, New York, NY 10020
www.howardpublishing.com

Library of Congress Cataloging-in-Publication Data

Ferguson, Mindy.
Hugs Bible reflections for women : 52 inspirational studies and stories to draw you closer to God / Mindy Ferguson.
p. cm.
Includes bibliographical references.
1. Christian women—Religious life. 2. Christian women—Religious life—Anecdotes. I. Title.
BV4527.F498 2008
242'.643—dc22

2008053146

ISBN 978-1-4165-8722-4
10 9 8 7 6 5 4 3 2 1

Manufactured in the United States of America

Edited by Between the Lines
Cover design by Tennille Paden
Interior design by Tennille Paden

The names of some individuals have been changed to protect their privacy.

Contents

May the words of my mouth
and the meditation of my heart
be pleasing in your sight,
O LORD,
my Rock and my Redeemer.

Psalm 19:14 NIV

Chapter One

Orchestrated Meeting

When I was upset and beside myself, you calmed me down and cheered me up.

Psalm 94:19 MSG

If only my eyes had windshield wipers. Tears blurred my vision as I turned onto the 405 freeway. How could a leadership meeting go so wrong? I had been caught completely off guard and walked into a whirlwind of false accusations and unrealistic expectations. When I was subsequently asked to step out of my ministry position for a time, I was stunned. I left the meeting hurt and confused. I wasn't in any condition to drive, but I just wanted to get home. My heart raced as I wept and relived the painful event. I blinked my eyes into focus and noticed a familiar personalized license plate on the car in front of me. It was my friend's car. Oh, how I needed a friend!

I honked my horn and flashed my headlights frantically until the car pulled to the shoulder of the road. I followed suit, turned off my engine, and ran along the freeway into the arms of two of my dearest friends. They hugged me for a moment before suggesting that we move to a safer location. We exited the highway and, since it was after dark, found a lighted parking lot. We all climbed into one car, where I relayed the evening's events. We talked, cried, and prayed together.

After a few minutes, my heart rate returned to normal and my tears slowed to a trickle. Relieved and grateful for their timely hugs, I asked my friends, who didn't live in the area, why they were in town. They had driven over to attend a special event, but their plans for a big night of fun had fallen apart when they were unable to find the event location. Their "we drove all the way down here for nothing" conversation had been interrupted by my honking horn and flashing lights.

Whenever I find myself in a state of despair, I remember that night on the 405 freeway. My friends' consoling hugs were a precious gift from God. He knew I would be in distress, and He sent two treasured friends to comfort me.

—Debbie Wong

Embracing God's Truth

As Debbie saw the familiar car and license plate on the freeway that night, she recognized that God had orchestrated her friends' presence precisely at her time of distress. He placed her friend's car in front of her so she would be able to receive the comfort and warm hugs she needed after a devastating meeting.

Have you ever had a friend show up at a time when you needed a warm hug or a friendly smile? If so, describe the circumstances.

____

____

____

Read Isaiah 46:10–11. What do you learn about God from these passages?

What additional information do you gain from Psalm 147:5?

God is powerful, and there is no limit to His knowledge and understanding. He can coordinate the circumstances of our lives to accomplish His divine purposes.

What additional encouragement do you find in Psalm 139:1–4, 13–16?

God knows all that has happened in your past; He is aware of the circumstances you find yourself in today; and He knows the challenges you will face tomorrow. He understands your thoughts before you even think them and your words before you say them. God created you, and you are precious to Him. You can take comfort in the realization that God anticipates your needs and is able to meet every one of them.

God orchestrated Debbie's meeting with friends on the 405. And as difficult as it was for her, He also allowed the painful events to unfold earlier that evening. Perhaps God had plans for Debbie other than the position she was in. Maybe someone else was supposed to lead that particular ministry at that time. Whatever the reasons behind that first meeting, neither of Debbie's two meetings that night happened without God's knowledge.

The next time you encounter a painful trial that you don't understand or run into a treasured friend when you're feeling discouraged, remember that God is the divine orchestrator. We don't always understand what He's doing, but He is always at work, in every meeting and situation, accomplishing His purposes.

Chapter Two

A Beautiful Completion

This is the way the holy women of the past who put their hope in God used to make themselves beautiful. They were submissive to their own husbands, like Sarah, who obeyed Abraham and called him her master. You are her daughters if you do what is right and do not give way to fear.

1 Peter 3:5–6

I turn sixty this year. I have been a widow for one year. And . . . I own cows. Ten years ago I lived in a big city with my beloved husband, Rick, and the cows were simply his weekend hobby. I never dreamed I'd become a cattle woman living on a ranch in the Hill Country of Texas without my husband.

Ten years ago I began to earnestly pray that my husband would become the spiritual leader of our household. Of course, I thought God would simply change Rick. But before my prayer could be answered, it was my heart that needed to undergo some adjustment.

One day my husband, a highly successful mechanical engineer, came home and announced that he wanted to move to our ranch. I thought he was joking at first. But when I realized he was serious, I struggled to know how to respond. After all, Rick was asking me to leave a twenty-year career as a social worker, lifelong friends, an active role in women's ministry at our church, and the modern conveniences of big-city life.

Within a few days I contacted our pastor's wife and sought her counsel. After explaining the circumstances, she asked me a predictable question: "Do you want to be a completer or a competer?" I had an intellectual understanding of obedience and submission. But I had to decide whether I really trusted God to bless me if I willingly submitted to my husband's lead, leaving behind my contented life in the city for a ranch where the nearest town had a population of only three thousand people.

All I could think about was what I would have to give up. I wanted to be "a completer," but I panicked at the thought of being just Rancher Rick's wife. So much of my identity was tied to my career, my friends, and the ministering I did at church. As I wondered how I could make such a move, I thought of Sarah from the Bible, a wonderful illustration of a submissive wife. She moved with her husband to an unknown land, leaving her hometown, her friends, and her family. I wondered if Sarah had struggled with some of the same feelings I was experiencing.

I read 1 Peter 3:5–6. Indeed, fear was my primary emotion. I knew Sarah had been blessed for her obedience. Hebrews 11:11 (NASB) tells us, "By faith even Sarah herself received ability to conceive, even beyond the proper time of life, since she considered Him faithful who had promised." So I trusted God, stepped out in faith, and followed my husband to the Flying D Ranch.

It was in the Texas Hill Country that God answered my prayer for Rick to be the spiritual leader of our home. In the city Rick had attended church and Sunday school with me, but he didn't actively study the Bible or lead family prayer time. I don't remember him ever talking about God's activity in his life. But after moving to the ranch, everything began to change.

First Rick volunteered to lead a couples Bible study with me. Then he began substitute teaching for a men's Sunday-school class. After we took a trip to Israel together, Rick frequently spoke to groups about Israel and the history of the Bible. On his initiative, we began a Bible study in our home, led by our former pastor from the city. In the years that followed, the group grew from fifteen to more than twenty-five men and women meeting at our home every week. At that point we moved the study to town, where it eventually reached an attendance level of fifty to sixty people. Whenever the pastor was out of town, Rick taught for him. My husband underwent an amazing transformation.

Two years after our move to the ranch, I asked Rick which memories of our time at the ranch were his favorites. He wrote his answer in a two-page Valentine's Day message. Here is a portion of his note:

> *One of the best ongoing memories is sharing our love for the Lord and the deepening of faith. The trip to Israel was one of the most memorable events on our religious journey. I know that there is much growth to come on my part, and I look forward to enjoying this with you. I really am thankful for your willingness to take the risk with me and move to the ranch. I know that this is a big adjustment for you and that the transition is more difficult for you than for me. . . . Honey, I love you very much and look forward to making many new and lasting memories with you.*

My beloved Rancher Rick spent six wonderful years on the Flying D Ranch making memories that I will forever cherish. We were blessed with an abundance of togetherness because my career was no longer in competition for my time with my husband. Rancher Rick had a true partner in life, and he was wonderfully content. I thank God that I know with certainty that my Rancher Rick finished well. Before acute respiratory distress syndrome took his life, he was working on a teaching message for our Bible study.

Ten years ago I asked God to make my husband the spiritual leader of our family. God asked me to be a submissive wife and to follow Rick to the ranch. I couldn't have known that my test of faith would be the situation through which God would answer my prayer, but it was. I thank God for giving me six wonderful years as Rancher Rick's wife and for showing me that I can trust in His Word. I didn't give way to my many fears. Like the holy women of the past, I put my hope in God, and He blessed me with a beautiful relationship with my husband that enabled him to become the man of faith God created him to be.

—Pam Durst

Embracing God's Truth

Pam was able to make the changes necessary for her husband's spiritual growth because she trusted God to bless her for submitting to her husband by putting his needs ahead of her own. Her willingness to live according to the principles in God's Word led to a beautiful transformation of her marriage.

Read 1 Peter 3:3–4. How does today's society define feminine beauty? Give examples.____

____

Read 1 Peter 3:5–6. You may not be married, but we all need to submit to God's authority to display the gentle and quiet spirit that is so valuable in His sight. What role does fear play in your struggle to submit to God's authority?

____

____

Read Psalm 34:1–5 and note what causes you to be radiant.

____

____

Follow the examples of Pam and Sarah: Don't give way to fear. Look to the Lord. Trust Him and submit to His Word. And don't be surprised when friends begin asking for your beauty secrets!

Chapter Three

Enlightening Flow

Let your light shine before men.

Matthew 5:16

After cleaning up what seemed like gallons of spilled nacho cheese sauce off the gym floor and picking up dozens of half-eaten hot dogs from the parking lot, I was tired and frustrated. My husband and I have rented a gym in an inner-city area on Thursday evenings for more than fifteen years. We open it up to the community for basketball, table games, and supper each week. We host between eighty and two hundred people ranging in age from infants to adults. We serve gang members, homeless people, school-aged children, and aspiring young athletes. Many come just to feast on the free hot dogs, nachos, and soda. Some play games, and others just hang out and visit. But everyone hears about Jesus, and our goal is to help them understand that He can make a difference in their daily lives.

This particular evening had been a rough one, with numerous scuffles and arguments. The gym got unusually messy, and as I mopped the floor and threw the last trash bag into the Dumpster, I prayed, "Lord, are we still supposed to be coming here? Are we being effective for You, or should we go and serve You somewhere else?" At last I shuffled out to our van. Much to my dismay, the vehicle was filled to capacity with young men needing a ride. Oh great, I thought, that's one more hour added to an already long ride home. I pulled myself up into the van next to my husband. He was smiling from ear to ear, thrilled with the opportunity to encourage and show God's love to the guys a little longer. The van reeked of smelly basketball players, and I was not smiling.

We started down the road, and I could hear the young men singing; but I was focused on my rapidly growing self-pity and didn't listen to their words. They were "flowing," which is a group form of rap. A group of people get a beat going and then take turns singing without breaking the rhyme and rhythm. It's entertaining when you're in the mood to listen, which I was not. But suddenly I realized they were flowing about us—joyfully singing about how we feed them and let them play basketball at the gym each week and (as if I didn't already feel guilty enough) how much we care about them.

My pity party ended abruptly, and I sat there in the smelly van with my heart bare before my Lord. I knew that serving God was never about me. But in a moment of discouragement, I had forgotten. *Lord*, I prayed silently, *thank You for flowing me back to reality.* I asked for God's forgiveness and felt a surge of encouragement as I prayed, *Lord, let my life be a constant "flow" about You so that people will know of Your love and Your salvation.*

—Tammy Harman

Embracing God's Truth

Tammy was discouraged after a long, exhausting day of inner-city ministry. She wondered if all of the effort and time was making a difference in the lives of those she and her husband served. But as she sat stewing in a van filled with smelly basketball players, God used their expression of love and gratitude to remind Tammy to keep her focus on serving Him and to love unconditionally, as God loves her.

Tammy asked God to let her life be a "flow" that continually displays His love and the salvation that is available through faith in Jesus. If your life were a song, what message do you think that song would communicate?

____

____

____

____

Read Matthew 5:13–16. Jesus said His followers are the salt of the earth. Salt stimulates our appetites and enhances the flavor of foods. Jesus also said that we are the light of the world. Our actions should shine so brightly with the love of God that people take notice.

According to verse 16, what is the reason we are to shine brightly by doing good works?

____

____

____

____

When we do good deeds in the name of Jesus, we are letting our light shine before the world. We are being salt when we whet their appetites for the gospel.

We are, in essence, allowing our lives to sing of His love so that we bring glory to our Father in heaven.

What message do you want your life-song to communicate?

____

____

____

____

____

Look back at your answer to the first question. If your song needs a little tweaking, ask God to help you change the message you convey.

Take a few minutes to write a few lines to your life-song. Write them down on an index card or a piece of paper and place it where you will see it often. Ask God to cause your light to shine and His love to "flow" in rhythmic harmony.

Chapter Four

Shepherding Voice

I am the good shepherd;
I know my sheep and my sheep know me.

John 10:14

I closed my Bible with a thump. "Lord, here's the deal. You said that Your sheep hear and know Your voice, but I can't tell when You're speaking to me. I never know when I'm hearing Your voice or just my own thoughts."

I drove to work and mulled over the problem. The logical conclusion kept pounding through my head: I must not be one of Your sheep.

At the office I gathered up a stack of outgoing mail from my desk and headed across campus to the post office. On autopilot, I trudged through the shade of oak trees, past flower gardens, and around a bubbling fountain. The verses I'd read that morning consumed my thoughts.

How can I tell when you're talking to me, God?

I opened the door to the student union building. A blast of air-conditioning jolted me from my reverie. I had no memory of the trek. Shaking my head, I determined to rid my mind of those distracting thoughts once and for all.

After depositing the office mail, I walked to the student bookstore across the hall. The store had a Russian textbook that I had wanted since I first saw it three weeks earlier. I pulled the book from the shelf and flipped through the pages. A smile tugged at my lips as my eyes caressed the Cyrillic characters. Ever since visiting Russia in the early 1990s, I longed to go back.

Taking the book to the checkout, I waited in line for my turn. I had an odd feeling that I shouldn't buy the book, but I shrugged it off, flipped open my checkbook, and scrawled, "University of North Texas Bookstore," on the appropriate line. The clerk punched some keys on her register, and her cash drawer opened. I poised the pen over the signature line.

Don't buy this book.

The words drummed through my head. The clerk's eyes glinted with impatience while she waited for my signature.

Don't buy this book.

Though the thought defied logic, it pestered me like my neighbor's yappy poodle. I cleared my throat and felt my face turning the color of a cherry Slurpee. "I'm sorry, but I'll need to cancel this purchase." I forced myself to meet the clerk's dagger eyes.

"Fine." The single word could have been a stainless-steel machete.

I swallowed hard, pushed the book across the counter, and hastened to the door. Outside, I tried to put some distance between me and my humiliation by speed-walking up the hill toward my office. Halfway to the top, I turned around.

This is stupid. I'm going to buy the book.

I continued the turn so that once again I faced my office.

Nope. Can't do it.

This is crazy! Anyone watching will wonder why this nutty woman is spinning in circles on the sidewalk. Crazy or not, I knew I couldn't buy the book.

Lord, I don't get it. I really want that book. Why can't I buy it?

"Hey, Sonjia," a girl's voice interrupted my silent prayer. "I thought that was you."

The girl attended my church, but we only ran into each other once in a great while. "I talked with your parents recently, and they said you wanted to go back to Russia."

I nodded, wondering where this was going.

"I have a Russian language textbook. It's the same one they sell in the campus bookstore. If you want it, I'd love to give it to you." She reached in her backpack and pulled out the coveted item.

Too amazed to manage more than a blurted "Thanks. That'd be great," I hugged the book and skipped the rest of the way to my office.

Okay, Lord, You've made your point. This little lamb does know Your voice. By the way, did I just hear a chuckle?

—Sonjia Bradshaw

Embracing God's Truth

As Sonjia struggled to know whether she was able to hear God speak, she clearly recognized His voice when she inexplicably understood that she was not supposed to purchase the Russian text book.

Believers in Jesus are members of His flock, and Scripture tells us that we should recognize when He is speaking.

Read John 10:1–3. What is the relationship between the Shepherd and His sheep?____

____

____

The Shepherd knows His sheep well. He knows their names, and they know His voice. That kind of knowing comes only through time spent together.

How much time did you spend with your Shepherd this week, interacting with Him through prayer, Bible study, or time in praise and worship?

____

____

Read John 10:4. Where do the sheep position themselves as they travel with their Shepherd?____

____

Do you usually ask God for direction before you act, seeking to follow your Shepherd, or do you tend to head out on your own, asking Him to correct you if you're heading in the wrong direction?_____________________________

____

____

As Jesus prepared His disciples for His departure, He wanted them to know that they would be able to hear from Him through the Holy Spirit. Read His words to His followers in John 16:12–15 and note the Holy Spirit's role in our communication with our Shepherd.

The Holy Spirit makes known to us the voice of our Shepherd. We need to spend time cultivating a relationship with God through prayer, Bible study, and worship. We need to seek His guidance and desire to follow Him. When we do, the Holy Spirit will lead us to the truth. We will come to know His voice and recognize when He is speaking.

Spend some time with the Shepherd this week. Slow down and listen for His voice. He may choose to speak through His Word, through circumstances, or, as with Sonjia, through an overwhelming sense that you are supposed to do something (or not do it). If you're unsure, ask Him to confirm His voice for you as He did with Sonjia. When He does, you'll know His voice—and don't be surprised if it puts a skip in your step too!

Chapter Five

The Pursuit of Today

But seek first his kingdom and his righteousness, and all these things will be given to you as well.

Matthew 6:33

I said good-bye to my dad—after his long battle with cancer—the same month my twins were born. The delightful, blond-headed pair was a perfectly timed gift from God to help bring healing and hope to my family. I'd been in an intense battle for my marriage and family for years, and those two new lives represented a promise of new beginnings. I was thankful for the opportunity to stay at home to raise them along with my two older children, whom I was homeschooling.

But just days after the twins' first birthday, it became clear that I would be left alone to raise my children, and our lives would take a dramatic turn. The first days and weeks felt dark and were filled with pain, loneliness, and fear. As the weeks passed, many decisions had to be made about work, schooling, and child care. The daily demands of running a household, generating income, and caring for the needs of four children seemed insurmountable. But I got through each day by praying and by reading, speaking, and breathing God's Word. I had claimed Matthew 6:33 as my life verse years earlier; now I really would have to choose to live it out every day.

I decided to put my life and the lives of my children fully into God's capable hands. I was determined not to hold anything back from Him. I did my best to seek God first in everything. I tithed, and I trusted Him with the results. There were days when sick children, car trouble, babysitting challenges, unpaid bills, or school needs brought discouragement and fear. Birthdays and holidays left me lonely and sad. I had moments when I wanted to lie down and give up. When I tried to look ahead to the next year or even the next week, fear and anxiety would steal my joy. But I realized that by living in the pain of the past or worrying about the future, I was giving away today with my children. I sensed that God was telling me to seek His kingdom and His righteousness first—His ways, His will, His forgiveness, His promises, His people, His fellowship, His Word, His heart, His healing, His hope. To do that, I had to seek Him one day at a time.

As I learned to live each day seeking Him fully and first, I found victory, joy, peace, healing, and hope. My todays weren't stolen. They were filled with living and thankfulness and gratitude. God has been faithful in providing for us. Not one time has a need gone unmet—not one time! My prayer journal is filled with records of needs met and prayers answered in miraculous ways.

The twins are now four years old, and God has provided income in a way that still allows me to be active in my role as a mother. In addition to meeting our daily needs, He has provided Christian schooling for my children, mentors and prayer partners to support me, ministry opportunities for our entire family, and fun and inexpensive family vacations. God is showing Himself faithful to me and to everyone who knows our family. Proverbs 31:25 says, "She is clothed with strength and dignity; she can laugh at the days to come." As I seek my heavenly Father and His kingdom, He clothes me in strength and dignity. I can laugh at the days to come because I know they are in His capable and trustworthy hands.

—Amy Kidd

Embracing God's Truth

When Amy began seeking God's kingdom and His righteousness on a daily basis, God was faithful in providing for the needs of her family. But perhaps God's greatest work was performed in Amy's heart as He brought her to a place where she has learned to enjoy today, clothed in strength and dignity as she relies on the Lord for her family's tomorrows.

In Jesus' famous Sermon on the Mount, He urged His followers not to worry about their basic needs but to seek the kingdom of God and His righteousness above all else. When we do, God will provide the things we need.

Read Matthew 6:25–32. What examples of God's faithful provision did Jesus give? ____________________

____

____

____

In Luke 12:29 Jesus said, "Do not set your heart on what you will eat or drink; do not worry about it." This is the only time Jesus is recorded as using this particular Greek word for worry. It means, "To hang suspended in midair." In other words, when we worry, we are so caught up in our anxiety over the needs of tomorrow that we are unable to enjoy our today.

Do you find yourself worrying about your future financial needs? If so, how does your anxiety over the future affect your ability to enjoy the present?

____

____

Read Matthew 6:33–34 and note Jesus' instructions.

Have you missed making memories with your family today because you were worrying about tomorrow? If so, focus your energy and attention on seeking God's kingdom and His righteousness. When you do, you'll be able to face your tomorrows with confidence, trusting that everything you need will be provided.

Chapter Six

Hearts Waiting

*Wait on the LORD; be of good courage,
and He shall strengthen your heart;
wait, I say, on the LORD!*

Psalm 27:14 NKJV

It was Valentine's Day. Just arriving home from work, I headed toward the bedroom, looking for Perry. The sight of two pink, chocolate-filled hearts lying on the bed stopped me in the doorway. I paused briefly, trying to compose myself before Perry turned around. He faced me with a self-satisfied grin. My husband had been a casualty of cutbacks at his company and had been out of work for a few weeks. Our cash flow had become severely restricted, and we were budgeting carefully; so the two small valentines—one for me and one for our daughter—were an extravagance. I felt a wave of nausea come over me as I realized that my news would soon overshadow the sweetness of the thoughtful candy hearts.

With leaden feet and an equally heavy heart, I entered the room. Leaning against the dresser, I stood silently with my coat still on and my purse in my hand. My eyes brimmed with tears, and Perry's smile sagged into a frown, his blue eyes clouding.

"I just lost my job," I blurted out as the tears began to flow.

"What happened?" Perry asked, with panic in his voice.

Dropping my purse, I slid slowly down the front of the dresser onto my knees and wept uncontrollably.

"Debbie, what happened?" Perry asked, my failure to answer panicking him even more.

I lifted my face and looked at him. "They didn't need me anymore. Last one in, first one out." I said through my tears. "I have a severance check in my purse."

Perry dropped to the bed, barely missing the pink hearts he had so lovingly placed there. For the next half hour, I relayed the events of the day. His shoulders drooped under the burden I had just placed there. In the end, I sat on the floor a red-eyed, tear-stained mess, repeating, "I'm so sorry."

Perry had soldiered through the recent, trying days, searching for another job, reviewing our finances, keeping a brave face to steady the family, but I always knew he was hanging on by a thread. I knew my job loss would only increase his burden. Finally he said, "Well, God has always taken care of us in the past. We just need to trust Him now." He pulled me to my feet, and we held each other for a few minutes. Later we sat down together and restructured our budget, adjusting for my severance check.

In the following weeks of searching for employment, Perry and I often took morning walks together. I still treasure the moments we shared during that difficult time as we focused on our future and tried to remain positive. I clung to the words of Psalm 27:14, doing my best to be strong and trust God as we waited for Him to provide the right job opportunities.

After a few months, Perry and I both found employment, and life returned to normal. I must admit, I still cannot look fondly on that Valentine's Day. But now when my life feels out of control, I remember the two pink candy hearts. They remind me of God's faithfulness to strengthen our two hearts as we supported each other and aspired to "be of good courage," while we waited upon the Lord.

—Debbie Acklin

Embracing God's Truth

Debbie will always remember that Valentine's Day when her husband's two pink, chocolate-filled hearts became visual representations of God's faithfulness to strengthen and more closely bind together their two hearts as they courageously waited for Him to provide the jobs they needed to support their family.

Can you recall a time when God seemed to wait a long time before responding to a need in your life? If so, explain.____________________________

____

The Bible is replete with stories of people who had to wait for God. One example is Nehemiah. He was a Jewish exile serving as cupbearer for the king of Persia. When a group of Jews came to the palace from Judah, Nehemiah asked about the conditions in Jerusalem. Read Nehemiah 1:3–4 and note Nehemiah's response to the news. ____________________________

____

Read Nehemiah 1:5–11. Nehemiah planned to approach the king and ask for permission to return to Jerusalem in order to rebuild the walls and repair the gates that had been destroyed. What did he ask God to do for him (verse 11)?

____

Nehemiah first learned about the conditions in Jerusalem during the Jewish month of Kislev (Nehemiah 1:1), which is during November and December in our calendar. Read Nehemiah 2:1–8. In what month did God provide an opportunity for Nehemiah to approach the king (verse 1)? ______________

____

Nisan falls during March and April in our calendar. So approximately how many months did Nehemiah wait for the Lord to grant his request? ______

How is Nehemiah described in verse 2?____________________________

____

Waiting on the Lord for an extended period of time can be discouraging. When God is slow (in our estimation) to work or answer our prayers, we often become weary of waiting. But Nehemiah was ready when God finally granted his request. Perhaps the four-month wait provided sufficient time for him to prayerfully prepare and strategize, because without hesitation, Nehemiah was able to tell the king how long he would need to complete the work. He also requested letters that would ensure his safety and enable him to acquire needed supplies.

Once in Jerusalem, Nehemiah organized a rebuilding project that is considered amazing even today. Despite heated opposition from surrounding governments and even some dissension among the Jews themselves, the walls were rebuilt in just fifty-two days.

Nehemiah's heart, which had been so burdened during his four-month wait, was strengthened, and he was empowered to accomplish an amazing feat for God's glory. What encouragement does Isaiah 40:28–31 offer for when we are discouraged while waiting for the Lord to work?

____

____

Whatever you're waiting for God to do in your life, be of good courage. When our hope is in the Lord, He will give strength to the weary and power to even the weakest of hearts.

Chapter Seven

The Phantom Rose Exchanger

No one has ever seen God.
But if we love each other,
God lives in us, and his love is brought
to full expression in us.

1 John 4:12 NLT

The summer of 1997 was perhaps the most tumultuous season of my life. After a seven-year battle with cancer, my husband, Dave, died on June 2. Two weeks later, our eighteen-year-old son, Andrew, graduated from high school. On June 22, I "celebrated" what would have been Dave's and my twenty-ninth wedding anniversary, and on June 25 Andrew left for the United States Air Force Academy to begin basic training. To top it off, the job that had been my passion for twenty-five years came to an end in August. My world seemed to be falling apart. Fortunately, I was surrounded by friends and family who supported me.

Autumn, usually my favorite time of year, loomed before me like a vast black hole. I was tormented by memories of school football games, holiday traditions, and cold rainy nights snuggled up with Dave in the house where we'd lived for twenty years. There I sat without a job, missing my husband and son more than I ever thought possible.

I attended Parents' Weekend at the Air Force Academy in September. It was the first time I'd seen my son since he'd left for the academy, and I was thrilled to visit with him and listen to his many stories about basic training. But as I sat by myself through all of the pomp and ceremony, the parades, the football game, and the other special events, devastation seemed to permeate deeper into my heart. Dave would have been so proud of Andrew. I cried the entire weekend.

The next "celebration" I faced was what would have been Dave's fifty-first birthday. I awoke that October morning with a dread of facing another significant milestone on my journey without my husband. I tried to tell myself it was just another day, but all I wanted to do was stay in bed. When I finally forced myself to go downstairs, someone knocked at the door. I was still in my flannel pajamas as I greeted a messenger from a local flower shop. He handed me a vase containing a single rosebud. The tiny card tucked into the greenery read, "From the Phantom Rose Exchanger." My heart felt as though it would break.

Before Dave and I were married, I lived in an apartment that we then shared after our wedding. When I moved in, Dave had given me a single rosebud. After the rose wilted, he sneaked in and replaced the dead rose with a fresh bud. He left a note: "From the Phantom Rose Exchanger." From that time on, whenever he gave me flowers, the card bore the same message.

I felt as though someone were standing on my chest. Tears gushed forth, and I couldn't catch my breath. I wondered if Dave had set this up before his death. *Surely he had been too sick to think this far ahead*, I thought. But so few people knew of his playful message that I couldn't imagine who would have arranged such an incredibly thoughtful surprise. My sister Randi suggested I call the florist, but I was too overwhelmed to make the call. I could barely speak. Randi took the phone number and offered to call for me. A few minutes later the phone rang. Randi was crying on the other end of the line. Through her sobs, she said that the florist couldn't tell her who sent the rose. He could only tell her where it came from. I held my breath as she explained that the rose had come from the United States Air Force Academy.

The thought of my eighteen-year-old son caring for his mom that way brought me to my knees. I had been at the point of total brokenness. Through Andrew's thoughtfulness I felt God's arms around me. I thanked my Lord for His incredible love and for the peace that suddenly flooded my heart. I knew God was in control and that I would be all right. I felt as though He were reaching down from heaven, holding my hand as I took my first steps toward healing.

—Donna Oiland

Embracing God's Truth

Andrew's thoughtful gift helped Donna recognize the depth of God's love for her. Often the most powerful demonstrations of God's love are felt when we choose to show sincere concern for the people around us.

Have you ever received an unexpected note or gift that, due to timing or other circumstances, caused you to recognize the depth of God's love for you?

If so, explain.____

____

____

____

Read 1 John 4:7–12. What was the ultimate expression of God's love (verse 9)?

____

____

____

God is love (1 John 4:8). When we are thoughtful and show true concern for people around us, God's love is expressed through our actions.

Is there someone in your life who needs to experience the depth of God's love? If so, what are some ways you can help them do that? ______________

____

____

____

Ask God to provide opportunities for you to reflect His love for that person.

Chapter Eight

Faithful Journey

By faith Abraham, when called to go to a place he would later receive as his inheritance, obeyed and went, even though he did not know where he was going.

Hebrews 11:8

Living in a rural Iowa community for over eight years, all our children had known was small-town life. Our family enjoyed living in a town where everyone knew our names and life was, for the most part, simple. But God interrupted our uncomplicated lives and sent us on a challenging adventure of faith.

As I sat in my office one day, enjoying the usual routine, my husband called unexpectedly and asked if he could come by and talk to me. When he arrived a few minutes later, the first words out of his mouth were, "I don't want you to say anything or answer me now. Just listen to what I have to say, and then pray about it before you give me an answer." I could feel my heart pounding in my chest as he told me that he had an opportunity to plant a new church in the Houston, Texas, area and that he was interested in pursuing it. My mind reeled. Planting a church in Houston meant moving away from our comfortable life in Iowa. We would have to leave our treasured friends and move our children from a sheltered small town to a large, fast-paced city. Needless to say, I didn't get much work done that afternoon.

After many conversations with trusted friends and family, numerous sessions at church-planting conferences, and hours of prayer, we decided that God wanted us to start a church in Texas. We dreaded telling our children about the move. When we finally sat them down and shared our plans, they reacted as we expected: lots of tears. We all cried and then cried some more. It was heartrending. All we could do was try to help our children understand that we had to trust God to know what was best for our family.

Soon we were on our way to Houston to look for a new place to call home. We drove around in circles for hours, day after day, looking at the same few areas. Our children were with us, and it's an understatement to say they weren't having much fun. When I was on the verge of tears and wondering if we really had heard God correctly, we pulled into a little convenience store for a restroom break. After we had all gotten reluctantly back into the car, I said, "Let's just take a minute to pray." The four of us sat in the car, right there in the gas station parking lot, and prayed together, asking God for guidance and patience.

We headed out once again and drove into an area that had begun to grow familiar. We saw many young families and decided to stop at a local store and ask for the name of the community. We felt sure we had found the right location for our church but soon learned that our sponsoring organization had another area in mind. My husband, however, was so convinced about the location that we were willing to start a church without the organization's support. Thankfully, God intervened and that wasn't necessary.

We contacted a local Realtor and began the long and exhausting process of looking at available homes. Unfortunately, before we found a place we liked, we had to go back to Iowa—and we didn't have the funds or the time for another house-hunting visit. We felt anxious and a little confused: our move to Houston was only a month away, and we were still without a home to go to. But we clung to our faith that God would provide.

Back in Iowa, our lives were filled with activity. We listed our house, said good-bye to longtime friends, and packed our belongings. The church where my husband had been preaching gave us their blessing when we announced our move. Amazingly, our house sold for three thousand dollars over the asking price to the first people who viewed it. As moving day approached, my husband and I searched frantically on the Internet for a house in Houston. We finally located two that looked like possibilities, so we asked his parents, who lived in the Houston area, to check them out. They did walk-throughs, gave us feedback, and sent a few pictures. By faith we made a decision and purchased a home off the Internet, without ever setting foot inside the door. I felt overwhelmed by the details, but God moved in incredible ways, confirming His will for us at every turn.

Moving day came, and we loaded all of our earthly belongings into a trailer. After a long, emotional day of driving, we finally made it to Houston. We were able to move into our new home and get settled just days before our girls started school.

The following Sunday we started our new church with the four members of our family. Over time, we had the privilege of worshiping every week with wonderful people we might never have known had we been unwilling to step out in faith and follow God. Through it all, our family learned to place our trust more fully in God—for He is the one who holds our future.

—Emma Liston

Embracing God's Truth

Whether God is moving you to a new city, prompting you to start a new church, or guiding you into a new career, obedience is seldom easy. Even though Emma had to leave her comfortable life in Iowa, she chose to trust that God had something planned for her and her family in Houston.

Read Genesis 12:1–5. Much like Emma and her husband, Abraham (originally named Abram) moved his family without even knowing where he was going. What did God tell Abram to leave behind? ________________

____

____

If God were to ask you to give up everything that is familiar and move to an unknown country, what would it be most difficult for you to leave behind?

____

____

How does Emma's story encourage you personally?__________________

____

____

Read Genesis 12:6–7. What happened when Abram arrived in Canaan (verse 7)?

____

____

Abram's faith was rewarded with a greater revelation of God's presence: God appeared to him. When we step out in faith, even though we don't understand what God has planned, we will experience a more intimate relationship with Him.

Is there a change that you sense God is prompting you to make at this time? If so, spend this week prayerfully considering what actions you need to take.

Chapter Nine

Mountains Moved

Who is this, robed in splendor, striding forward in the greatness of his strength? "It is I, speaking in righteousness, mighty to save."

Isaiah 63:1

When my husband, Brad, came home from work one day and told me that he would be going on a mission trip to central India, I was genuinely thrilled. Brad was a youth pastor then, and he'd traveled to Mexico many times, but I never dreamed either of us would have the opportunity to travel to the other side of the world.

In the months that followed, we were busy preparing for his trip. He got immunizations, applied for a visa, and purchased a number of items he would need during his travels. As our church staff and congregation also began to prepare for the group trip, I learned more about the risks and dangers of traveling to central India to spread the gospel. I was assured that Brad would have a guard with him at all times (which brought me more concern than comfort), and I remembered hearing that India was considered a country hostile toward Christians. I also learned that only 2 percent of the population at that time was Christian, and persecution was common.

A week before Brad's scheduled departure, I was consumed by fear for his safety. Our daughter was three years old, and our son was six. Every time I looked at them, I thought, *What if something happens to their daddy? What if something happens to my husband!?* Despite my efforts to console myself, I began to dread the day he was scheduled to leave. I wanted to support him, and I knew he was at peace with his decision, but I was terrified by the thought of losing him.

I drove Brad to the airport and tried to be the strong minister's wife that I thought I should be. I didn't want to say good-bye, but by God's grace I kept my composure. I was so preoccupied by praying for his safety that I didn't even think to pray for the people whose lives might be changed by his work there.

During the first week of his trip, I spent a lot of time on my knees in our bedroom, praying earnestly for his safe return. Brad began sending e-mails relaying amazing stories about people accepting Christ even though it meant they would be disowned by their families. He wrote about the people he'd met who had survived horrific persecution but still chose to boldly proclaim Christ as their Lord.

I went to the midweek service at our church, and we sang about our Savior's ability to move mountains and about the fact that our God is mighty to save. I knew those words were true. I knew that God was powerful enough to protect my husband, and I had been reading frequent accounts of His "moving mountains" on the other side of the world, in a country where only a tiny percentage of the people knew Him as Lord.

My prayers during my husband's second week in India changed dramatically. I still spent time on my knees, but now my prayers were for the people who were hearing the gospel for the first time and those who were giving up everything to follow Jesus. I prayed for those who would suffer torture or even death because of their professions of faith.

I was relieved when God brought Brad back home, safe and unharmed. The next time I got down on my knees, it was to express the gratitude I felt, not only for God's faithfulness in returning my husband, but also for His power to move mountains of fear—both in my heart and in the hearts of all those in India who had accepted Him as Savior. Our God truly is mighty to save.

—*Tanya Pembleton*

Embracing God's Truth

Tanya's fear for her husband's safety overshadowed the purpose of his mission trip. But as she heard about the mighty way God was moving in the hearts of the Indian people, the mountain of fear that stood so ominously before her was moved, and her focus became aligned with God's will and with the purpose of the trip: reaching the people of India with the message of salvation through Jesus Christ.

People in your community need to hear the gospel too. Are there any mountains of fear that keep you from reaching out to your family, friends, or neighbors with the message of salvation through Jesus Christ?

____

____

____

____

Read Matthew 17:14–20. What was the reason Jesus gave for His disciples' inability to cast out the evil spirit? ______________________________

____

____

____

Look at Matthew 10:1. What authority did Jesus give to His disciples?

____

____

____

The disciples had seen Jesus heal people and cast out demons. He gave them authority to do the same. Yet they struggled to have faith in Jesus' power to heal through them. Look again at Matthew 17:20. What did Jesus say would happen if they had faith the size of a mustard seed?____________________

____

____

____

It seems a tall order to expect people to declare faith in Jesus when they know they'll be persecuted and possibly tortured or even killed. It may seem unrealistic to expect a wife with young children to pray more earnestly for the salvation of people living on a different continent than for the safety of her husband. But what seems impossible is possible when we operate under God's authority and rely on His power.

Read Matthew 28:16–20. Jesus has been given all authority in heaven and on earth, and He has commissioned us to go and make disciples of all nations. He tells us He will be with us—whether we travel to a country like India or we just talk to a neighbor down the street.

Look back at your answer to the first question above. Ask God to move the mountains of fear that have kept you from sharing the gospel with people around you. Rely on His power. For when your faith is in God's ability to work through you, mountains will move, and nothing will be impossible. Our Lord is mighty to save.

Chapter Ten

Loving In-Laws

Be completely humble and gentle; be patient, bearing with one another in love.

Ephesians 4:2

When I first began dating the man who would become my husband, I enjoyed spending time with his parents. They were warm and fun. His mom was a wonderful cook and took joy in preparing lavish meals. She always made me feel welcome and accepted me with open arms.

After Guy and I married, I noticed subtle changes in my relationship with his mother. Guy and I made decisions about our home life that were different from the decisions my in-laws had made, and those differences seemed to create distance in our relationship with them. When our sons were born, the approach Guy and I took toward parenting caused the divide to widen.

I prayed for a closer relationship with my mother-in-law. I truly wanted to be close to her, but as the years passed, I prayed with less enthusiasm. We still saw each other, but I made little effort to improve our relationship. My focus was on my own family, which was thriving, and my days were full of purpose.

When my father-in-law died, my relationship with my mother-in-law grew even more distant. She quickly remarried, and my husband and I both struggled to accept her choice. As a result, the gap in our relationship grew so wide that I did not think it could be bridged.

When my mother-in-law's health began to decline and it became evident that her remaining time on this earth would be short, I was heavily involved in women's ministry at my church, and my husband's business schedule was hectic. We also had a son in college, and our youngest was a senior in high school. Despite my responsibilities, I felt God urging me to make my mother-in-law a priority. As I analyzed our relationship, I had to admit that she had always accepted me just the way I was. I was the one who had struggled to accept her. I knew I would not have another chance to show love to her, so I made the time—and God did a wonderful thing. He softened my heart, and I was able to love my mother-in-law more deeply than I ever thought possible. I even had the blessing of seeing her come to Christ in the weeks before her death. While I regret the lost years, I am grateful for the many special moments we shared in her final days and the healing of our relationship that God provided.

Today I am a mother-in-law. It's a new journey that I am sure will come with a few bumps in the road. But I seek God's strength and wisdom so I can have the kind of relationship with my daughters-in-law that He wants for us.

—Robin Lipe

Embracing God's Truth

Robin struggled to have a close connection with her mother-in-law. Yet when she allowed God to soften her heart, she was able to overcome the differences that had created distance in their relationship. As she approaches the complexities of an in-law relationship from a new perspective, she is asking God to help her to develop a strong, accepting, and loving relationship with her daughter-in-law.

Are there any in-laws you struggle to accept and love? If so, how do you think your differences in culture, tradition, or philosophy affect your relationship?

____

The biblical story of Naomi and Ruth is a wonderful example of a loving in-law relationship between two women from different cultures and backgrounds. Naomi was an Israelite woman who moved from Judah to Moab with her husband to escape a famine. While in Moab, Naomi's two sons married Moabite women, one of whom was Ruth.

Decades earlier, some other Israelites had a memorable encounter with some women of Moab. Read Numbers 25:1–3 and note what preconceived notions or concerns Naomi might have harbored that could have affected her in-law relationships.

Read Ruth 1:5–9. According to verse 8, how had Ruth and Orpah treated Naomi?____

____

____

When Naomi instructed her daughters-in-law to return to their mother's house, what was her hope for the two of them?____________________________

____

____

Naomi had the women's best interests at heart. She wanted what she thought was best for her daughters-in-law. What can you conclude about Ruth and Naomi's relationship from the scene described in Ruth 1:10–18? __________

Ruth appears to have developed a deep love for Naomi despite their cultural and religious differences. What insight into Naomi's feelings toward Ruth do you gain from the way Naomi addresses Ruth in Ruth 2:2? ____________

Over the years, Naomi and Ruth had evidently developed a relationship more like that of a mother and daughter. As you seek to develop close relationships with the in-laws in your life, what are some ways that you can help bridge cultural differences and respect traditions that might be different from your own? ____________

Look again at Ruth 1:16. As Ruth begged Naomi to allow her to travel back to Judah with her, Ruth made it clear that she not only wanted to be a part of Naomi's family, but she also wanted Naomi's God to be her God.

After returning to Judah with Naomi, Ruth married a man named Boaz. Matthew chapter 1 records the genealogy of Jesus Christ. Whose names appear in verse 5? ____________

Not only did Naomi build a strong relationship with her daughters-in-law, despite cultural and religious differences, but she also obviously enriched Ruth's life so dramatically that Ruth chose to leave behind the religious views of her ancestors and follow the God of Israel.

Take a moment to pray that God will give you a deep and sincere love for the in-laws (even the ones listed in the first question above) in your life. Ask Him to help you be humble and gentle as you interact with them, and to be patient with their weaknesses so that you can reflect the love of Christ.

Chapter Eleven

Compassion at Work

The LORD is good to all;
he has compassion on all he has made.

Psalm 145:9

Due to a combination of bad choices and dysfunctions in my family, I left home when I was fourteen years old. It took me a long time to learn how to manage my money. I vividly recall a time when, at age fifteen, I had run completely out of money. I didn't have any food in my pantry. Payday was several days away, and I had no idea where to turn. I went for days without eating. When I finally received my paycheck, I immediately cashed it and walked to the nearest grocery store. I bought as much food as I could afford. In my excitement, I didn't consider how I would transport all of my purchases. The brown paper bags were packed to the brim. I started walking to my apartment about a mile away, but it wasn't long before the cumbersome sacks began to break open. I was horrified as all of my groceries fell to the ground. Disheartened and fearful for the future, I sat down on the side of the road and sobbed like a helpless child.

After a few minutes, a young couple in a van stopped and asked if they could help me. Desperate and distraught, I didn't refuse. They helped pick up all of my items. They tried their best to console me as we drove to my apartment and they helped me carry my purchases inside. The young woman encouraged me and lovingly told me that God loved me and had a plan for my life.

Over the course of the next thirteen years, I was comforted often when I reflected on that young woman's words. At the age of twenty-eight, I surrendered my life to Christ. I recognized that He had been wooing me since that day thirteen years earlier when He sent His messengers to help me, to assure me of His love, and to demonstrate His compassion by sacrificing their time to stop and help me when I was distraught and afraid.

—Tina Roeder

Embracing God's Truth

Tina felt helpless and afraid as she sat at the side of the road with all of the groceries she could afford scattered on the ground. Because a young couple was willing to sacrifice their time to help, they communicated to her God's compassion and love, which ministered to Tina's heart and eventually drew her into a relationship with her Savior.

On a typical day, most of us hurry from place to place checking off tasks from our to-do lists. Can you think of a time when you interrupted your schedule or rearranged your agenda to stop and help a stranger in need? If so, explain. If not, how do you think you would have responded to seeing Tina? ______________________________

____

____

In our busy society it seems we're becoming more and more focused on ourselves and less compassionate about (or even aware of) the needs of people around us. What does Deuteronomy 15:11 tell us?____________________

____

____

____

____

Read Philippians 2:1–4. How should we, as members of the body of Christ, treat people around us?____

____

____

____

____

Compassion means having pity for the suffering of other people, and wanting to help them. Jesus demonstrated God's compassion by sacrificing His life on the cross for our sins. We should be like-minded, sacrificing for the needs of others.

It's often easier to write a check and give it to the benevolence fund at our church than it is to sacrifice our time to help someone who is distraught or unable to care for herself. Yet James 1:27 tell us, "Religion that God our Father accepts as pure and faultless is this: to look after orphans and widows in their distress."

In the space below, list anyone you currently are aware of who is struggling financially or whose basic needs are not being met:

____

____

____

Ask God to fill your heart with compassion—not just pity for those who are suffering but a strong desire to do something to help them. Take a moment to review the names you've listed above. What are some ways you could help meet their needs? ______________________________

____

____

____

____

____

Practice compassion this week. Do what you can to meet one of the needs you've listed. Ask God to continually fill your heart with compassion and to provide opportunities for you to act upon it.

Chapter Twelve

Divine Help and Heaven-Bound Kisses

Samuel took a stone and set it up between Mizpah and Shen. He named it Ebenezer, saying, "Thus far has the LORD helped us."

1 Samuel 7:12

Our grandchildren were devastated by the loss of their baby brother. It was unthinkable for all of us. It was a cold day in January 2004 when baby Ryan's infant body, only eighty days old, shut down. Doctors assured our family that sudden infant death syndrome (SIDS) cannot be prevented or predicted. There was nothing we could have done.

The days following our grandson's death were filled not only with funeral arrangements and play dates for the other children at Grandma's house but also with many questions about the best way to help our young grandchildren say good-bye to baby Ryan. My heart broke as they loudly insisted that they were not ready to say good-bye. They wanted their brother to come back home.

One day as I was hugging and blowing kisses to the kids as they went out the door, I silently prayed, *Lord, help me to help them through this terrifying and heartrending time. Help us all to say good-bye with love.* That evening I came up with the idea of having a balloon release at the graveside with the children. I thought it might be a tangible way for them to say good-bye and release baby Ryan to God's care in heaven. Their parents liked the idea, and we bought the balloons.

At the funeral, in addition to an array of flowers and toys, the church was decorated with balloons in pastel colors. As I sat in a pew during the service, I kept crying out to God, asking for help to get through the most difficult loss of my life. I wanted to offer a tribute to my grandson, but no words came to mind. My heart ached as we headed toward the cemetery.

Once there, each grandchild was given a balloon to release. The girls began to protest. "I don't want to say good-bye. I want to give him hugs and kisses."

Spontaneously, I replied, "Send baby Ryan hugs and kisses on your balloons. He'll like getting your hugs and kisses in heaven."

The children instantly responded to my suggestion, planting several hugs and kisses on each of their balloons and then releasing them to float peacefully up into the winter sky. As we watched the balloons disappear out of sight, my grandson yelled, "Look! Jesus made a cross in the sky with his finger! Jesus is happy with us for flying our hugs and kisses to heaven for baby Ryan!"

I choked back tears as I looked up to the sky. The clouds had formed a cross. "Yes," I said to them through tears. "Jesus and baby Ryan are happy with you for flying your hugs and kisses to heaven."

I breathed a deep sigh of relief and silently praised God for answering my prayers for help. We had honored our grandbaby, and the children had been reassured of Jesus' loving care for baby Ryan. God helped all of us begin healing that day as we sent our hugs and kisses toward heaven and saw the comforting image of a billowy cross divinely painted across the sky.

—Jewel Sample

Embracing God's Truth

Jewel cried out for the Lord to help her as she tried to come up with a healing and meaningful way for her grandchildren to say good-bye to their baby brother. God was faithful not only to give her creativity for the idea of the balloon release but also to comfort those little ones with His presence as the clouds formed the shape of a cross high above the cemetery. She knew that God had helped her, just as she had requested.

When was the last time you encountered a situation that left you crying out to God for help? ______________________________________

____

____

One time, when the people of Israel gathered in Mizpah to rededicate themselves to the Lord, their enemies, the Philistines, came to attack them.

Read 1 Samuel 7:7–11. What did the people urge Samuel to keep doing (verse 8)? ____

____

____

How did God respond to Samuel's cries for help? ____________________

____

____

God was faithful to help His people and save them from the Philistines. God will also help us when we need rescuing. Whether you're battling fear or financial hardship or dealing with a heartbreaking tragedy, God wants to be your source of help.

Look up the following passages and note the descriptions of God as helper:

Deuteronomy 33:26–27__________________________________

2 Samuel 22:29–31 _____________________________________

Proverbs 18:10____

Read 1 Samuel 7:12. After God was faithful to help His people, what did Samuel do? _______________________________________

____

As Jewel walked away from the cemetery that day, she may not have known how she would deal with the many phases of grieving and healing that yet awaited her, but she knew with certainty that so far the Lord had indeed helped her.

Take a moment to reflect on God's faithfulness to carry you through illness or tragedy or battles in the past. Write down some moments when you could say with certainty, "Thus far has the Lord helped [me]": ________________

____

____

Is there a crisis you're facing right now? If so, explain. ________________

____

____

Whenever you face unspeakable grief or battle against unthinkable odds, remember the stone Samuel erected at Mizpah. Cry out to God. Ebenezer means "stone of [divine] help." Whether God rides on the heavens to help you (Deuteronomy 33:26), turns darkness to light (2 Samuel 22:29), or becomes a tower of safety (Proverbs 18:10), you can anticipate divine help. Be ready to set up your Ebenezer stone. Sometimes help comes in the form of strength and courage during battle. And sometimes it comes in the form of a comforting, billowy cross when we turn our hearts and our eyes heavenward.

Chapter Thirteen

Crossing Jordan

As soon as the priests who carried the ark reached the Jordan and their feet touched the water's edge, the water from upstream stopped flowing.

Joshua 3:15–16

Often the most challenging part of walking along a new path with God is the first step. I was on the staff of a church in Houston, Texas, serving God in a variety of roles. I had written a couple of Bible studies and had spoken at a few women's events, and my passion for women's ministry began to stir a deep longing to focus my time and energy in that area. Although I was actively serving God in my position with the church, I began to feel like I was wandering in the desert, much like the Israelites had done on their way to the Promised Land.

One morning I sat in my upstairs study, drinking my coffee and prayerfully reading about the Israelites' wanderings. My heart was heavy as I asked God when my desert season would be over. I read Deuteronomy 2:7, "The Lord your God has blessed you in all the work of your hands. He has watched over your journey through this vast desert. These forty years the LORD your God has been with you, and you have not lacked anything."

My heart began to pound, for it seemed that God was speaking through His Word. I praised Him, for He had indeed blessed my work and had continually made His presence known to me throughout my ministry. Suddenly the word *forty* seemed to lift off the page. I began to pray, *Lord, are you telling me that my time in the desert is forty years? That can't be right. I'd be almost eighty years old. Oh, please don't tell me I will be wandering for forty years!*

Forty still screamed at me from the page of my Bible. *Maybe He means forty months,* I thought as I began calculating. My fortieth month with the church would be April 2005. I sensed a quickening in my spirit as I asked the Lord if April 2005 was correct. Feeling the date was confirmed, I said, "April 2005, I can do that." I continued, "That's sixteen more months. Okay, Lord."

I started to close my Bible, but the words *forty years* began to reverberate in my mind. After rereading the passage several times, I cried out to God: "Lord, I don't understand. How can it be forty months and forty years? I don't understand what You're saying!" Then the realization washed over me like a soaking rain: I would be forty years old in April 2005!

I dropped to my knees beside the comfortable futon where I met with God regularly. After several seconds of stunned silence, I thought, Only God could make the fortieth month also be my fortieth year. Trembling, I marked the date in my prayer journal. I later told my husband and a few trusted friends while I waited confidently and the months passed.

Fear began to grip me as my fortieth birthday approached. I wondered if I had misunderstood God or merely imagined that He'd spoken. Although my speaking engagements were increasing, all of the fees were being used to fund the ministry. My husband, Mark, and I reviewed our finances. We prayed about how we could get by if I quit my job and focused on ministry full-time—without a salary—but we didn't see how we could manage.

In late March we received notification that Mark had a retirement account with a former employer. For some reason we had no record of the account. The balance was equal to half my annual salary at the church. After reviewing the statement, Mark said, "I think we should cash this in. It would enable you to focus on building the ministry for six months."

I struggled to accept his offer. I asked God to please confirm His will, but my birthday came and went without any confirmation. Days dragged by as I waited for God to move. The last week of April came, and I struggled through Monday and Tuesday, begging God for confirmation. Wednesday, April 27, was the last day the senior pastor (and my boss) would be in the office that month. As I sat down at my desk that morning, the choice seemed simple: I believed God had spoken to me through His Word sixteen months earlier, and therefore I had no choice but to obey what He said.

I stepped out in faith just as the Israelites had when their priests stepped into the Jordan River en route to their Promised Land.

God parted my Jordan River when, six months after leaving the church (almost to the day), I signed a contract to publish my first Bible study. I've taken many more steps of faith, and God has been faithful to provide throughout my journey in ministry, but the most challenging part was that first step.

—Mindy Ferguson

Embracing God's Truth

I struggled with fear and doubt as I aspired to follow God and obey what I believed He had told me to do through His Word. When I chose to step out in faith, God was faithful to provide for my needs and ultimately confirmed that I had heard Him correctly. But the confirmation came after I took that first step of faith.

The Israelites wandered in the desert for forty years because they had been unwilling to cross the Jordan River and trust God to give them victory over the people then living in the Promised Land (Numbers 14:33–34).

Read Exodus 33:1–2 and note what God had promised to do for His people. ____

____

As the Israelites stood at the shore of the Jordan River a second time, led by Joshua, they had to decide whether they believed that God would do what He had said He would do.

What instructions did God give the Israelites in Joshua 3:9–13?__________

____

According to verse 13, when would the Israelites know that God would drive their enemies out of the land? ______________________________

____

When we sense God telling us to do something, we usually want Him to confirm that He will move on our behalf before we act. But God had told the Israelites forty years earlier that He would give them the land. And, as is often the case with us today, they had to act before they would receive confirmation that He was indeed "living among them" and would fulfill His promise.

Read Joshua 3:14–17. The waters of the Jordan were at flood stage. The ark of the covenant was a large, sacred chest covered in pure gold, and it was quite heavy. Had the waters not parted, the priests probably would have drowned as they attempted to carry the ark across the river. But they chose to take God at His word and step out in faith. As their feet touched the water and it stopped flowing, the God of all the Earth confirmed that He would drive out the nations before them.

Do you sense God moving you along a new path right now? If so, what are the circumstances? ______________________________

____

Don't be surprised if He is silent as you wrestle with fear and doubt at the shore of your Jordan River. For it is often only after you obey that He removes the obstacles and confirms the direction. Ask Him for the courage to take the first step.

Chapter Fourteen

Hooligan's Hope

Love your enemies and
pray for those who persecute you.

Matthew 5:44

Here we go again, I thought as I started down the stairway to take my trash to its rightful place at the end of the parking lot. Eight young men wearing oversized pants and T-shirts were standing in a huddle about halfway between the Dumpster and my apartment. The boys were laughing and shoving one another in fun.

Armed with only courage, I continued across the lot, wondering what verbal assaults awaited me. The hooligans blocked my path. As I tried to pass, the group entertained themselves by running in circles around me. I took a deep breath, stopped, and whispered a prayer. At that moment one of the boys reached over and grabbed a necklace I was wearing. It had the words *Walking with God* printed on the front. Mocking me, he laughed and asked, "Are you walking with God?"

"Yes," I said.

"She's walking with God to the trash!" he sarcastically shouted to the others in the group.

In an effort to disguise my distress, I calmly invited him to come along. "You can hop in with this trash!" I said, pretending to join in the fun. After I put my garbage bag into the Dumpster, the boy followed me, distancing himself from the rest of the group. He quietly asked, "Do you walk with God?"

"Sure," I said. "You can walk with God too."

"Nah," he quickly replied. "I gave up on that stuff a long time ago."

"He wants you to walk with Him," I said as the young man turned to walk back to his friends. Laughter erupted from the group as I made my way back to my apartment.

Two days later there was a knock at my door. As I peered through the peephole, I could see the young man standing on my porch. I cautiously opened the door. "My girlfriend is pregnant," he said, staring down at his shoes.

I motioned for him to come inside. We talked for a while, and I gave him a list of phone numbers for organizations that could help his girlfriend.

"I have no money," he mumbled, once again looking down at his shoes.

I reminded him that he had expensive wheel rims and an obnoxiously loud stereo in his car that could be sold if he needed money. When he objected, I reminded him that he'd gotten into his predicament because he wanted to act like a man. "Be one," I said. "And get a pair of pants that fit!"

As he was leaving, he paused on the stairwell, turned and said, "My name is Jerod."

"I'm Annette," I said as I waved good-bye.

A few days later Jerod returned to my door. This time he had his girlfriend, Rachel, with him. I invited them inside, and Rachel thanked me for the information I'd given Jerod. Because of circumstances in Rachel's home life, the couple planned to go and live with Jerod's grandmother in another state as soon as Rachel finished high school. Jerod grimaced and said, "Man, Maw is gonna make us go to church twice a week."

"Good," I said. "You need it!"

The next time I saw Jerod, he had taken a job at a local department store and had sold his expensive wheel rims and car stereo. For the next week, whenever Jerod or Rachel walked past my apartment, I would open the door and teasingly shout out threats like, "You'd better hope you do the right thing for this baby," or "You'd better hope you get to work on time today." To Rachel I shouted, "I hope you studied for those finals!" The couple always laughed and waved.

Sadly, Jerod and Rachel once again appeared on my front porch about a week before their scheduled departure. Rachel's home situation had deteriorated, and it was apparent that the couple needed to leave immediately. But Jerod wasn't expecting his paycheck for another three days.

Despite his objections, I went online and took a cash advance on my next disability check. I gave Jerod my bank card and told him to go to the nearest ATM and get the money he needed. After promising to pay me back, Jerod and Rachel agreed. "I'll do her proud," he said as he started down the stairway.

"I know, I know. Walk with God," I said as I waved good-bye.

Before the couple reached the bottom of the stairs, I called Jerod back. I lifted the *Walking with God* necklace from around my neck and gave it to him. "This belongs to you now," I said.

"I will give it to the baby one day and tell her about you," Jerod said with a smile.

"Yeah, get going!" I said as I choked back tears.

Over the months that followed, Jerod called a few times and sent money in the mail to repay me. One day he called to tell me that amniocentesis had revealed that they were having a baby girl. His voice cracked as he told me the test also revealed she would be born with Down syndrome. Pain ripped through my heart. After a moment I gathered myself and told him, “God doesn’t make mistakes, Jerod. He trusts you and Rachel with this little girl.”

“I love them both,” he said. “I don’t care that the baby may have problems.”

“I know,” I said. “Keep walking with God, you hear?”

“I will, Miss Annette,” he whispered as he hung up the phone.

Precious baby Hope (named after my teasing threats) was born healthy. Indeed different, but aren’t we all? Jerod, Rachel, and Hope are doing well. Jerod is enrolled in college and intends to become an accountant someday. The last time I spoke with him, his grandmother was dragging them all to church *three* times a week.

—Annette Sanko

Embracing God’s Truth

Annette chose to react with love rather than spite when the young man who had mocked her sought her help. Her genuine concern for him and his girlfriend provided a means for the young couple to find for themselves the hope that walking with God can bring.

True love is expressed when we have a person’s best interests at heart, even when that person has hurt our feelings or treated us with contempt. Read Matthew 5:43–47. According to verse 44, how are we to treat our enemies?

____

Is there someone you currently find difficult to love? If so, what is it about that person that you are struggling to accept? ____________________________

____

Read Matthew 5:48. None of us can truly be perfect. But when we wholeheartedly commit to treating others in a way that is in harmony with God’s will, we reflect God’s love to the world around us. Take a few minutes to pray that God will bless the man or woman you listed above. The next time you’re around this person, ask God to help you reflect His love.

Chapter Fifteen

Grocery Money

My God will meet all your needs according to his glorious riches in Christ Jesus.

Philippians 4:19

We were newlyweds, still in college. My husband, Bo, had a job, but I was still looking for work. Meeting our expenses each month was a challenge. One Saturday, as we were discussing how we could pay for groceries, the phone rang.

Bo answered. When he hung up, he said, "That was Roger. He wants me to do some work for him at the shop today."

Roger owned a whetstone-cutting shop in the area and called Bo occasionally when they needed some extra help. Relieved to momentarily escape the stressful prospect of grocery shopping with only a few dollars, I told him that shopping could wait until that evening.

Kissing me as he stepped out the door, Bo said, "Be ready by five-thirty so we can shop, get home, and eat at a decent hour."

I decided to clean while he was gone. The living room was small enough that I could reach the television while sitting on the sofa. Our dining room was barely large enough for a table and four chairs, and I could clean all of the appliances in our tiny kitchen while standing still. Needless to say, cleaning didn't take long.

As I ran my dust cloth over a framed plaque of Philippians 4:19 that was hanging by the front door, I thought about the call Bo had received from Roger. I smiled as I recognized the call as God's way of taking care of us. I'd never paid much attention to God's provision in my life. My recognition of His care brought me comfort as I finished cleaning and waited for Bo to return.

Bo walked in later that evening filthy and exhausted, but he was excited because Roger had paid him $15.44 in cash for the day. After he cleaned up, Bo was eager to go shopping, so we headed out. By the time we pulled into the store parking lot, our stomachs were growling. Knowing that we didn't have much more than Bo had earned that day, we selected our purchases carefully. We didn't keep a running total of our costs, but only necessities were placed in the shopping cart.

We approached the checkout counter and took one last inventory of our cart. Satisfied that we had what we needed, we placed the items on the counter. The clerk tallied our bill and handed it to Bo. He stood silently in front of the counter, looking at the receipt for a moment, and then turned with a look of amazement on his face as he quoted the total: "Fifteen dollars and forty-four cents."

—*Kathryn Graves*

Embracing God's Truth

Bo and Kathy needed money to buy food. Because Bo's earnings were the exact amount needed for groceries, they recognized that the work at the whetstone shop had been God's provision. The young couple experienced the rich blessing of recognizing the personal way God cares for His children.

A widow who lived in a town named Zarephath once experienced God's provision in a personal and specific way too. Read 1 Kings 17:7–16.

The widow had only enough oil and flour to prepare one last meal. Yet how long did God say the oil and flour would last (verse 14)? ______________

____

____

____

____

According to 1 Kings 18:1, how long did the land endure drought?

____

____

____

____

____

Not only did the widow and her family have food to eat every day during the years of drought, but they also had enough for the prophet Elijah.

Has there been a time when God supplied a specific need in your life? If so, describe the circumstances.______________________________

____

____

Kathy and Bo knew that God was the source of their grocery money. And when the drought ended around the same time that the widow's flour was used up and her oil ran dry, I imagine she recognized that God had been the source of every one of the meals she and her family had eaten during those dry years.

Take a moment to tell God how thankful you are for His faithful provision. Ask Him to help you be more aware of His activity on your behalf.

Chapter Sixteen

Sustaining Praise

O Lord, open my lips,
and my mouth will declare your praise.

Psalm 51:15

Moving Dad into a nursing home was painfully difficult. He wasn't sick, but he had become incapacitated to the point where he needed full-time skilled nursing care. I'd worked in a nursing home, and I thought that I was prepared, but all of my experience could not have equipped me to deal with the sadness I felt as we moved Dad into the home to live among many fragile and dying people.

Each day, as I went to see him, I had to ask God for the grace and strength to do whatever my dad needed without revealing the deep sorrow that seemed to crush my heart each time I walked down the long corridor toward his room. There were days when I begged God to conceal the tears that would inevitably roll down my cheeks. It just didn't seem possible that my father belonged in that environment.

Because Dad's room was at the end of the hall, I became familiar with many of his neighbors, whom I passed on my way to visit him. One of the oldest residents used to sit in her wheelchair, positioned unobtrusively next to the nursing station, where she watched the nurses, visitors, and other residents. Most of the time she was preoccupied and mumbled incoherently, as if she were carrying on a conversation with herself. Yet surprisingly, when someone walked by, she would raise her head to greet him or her with a smile and articulately speak the same words to each one: "Taste and see that the LORD is good" (Psalm 34:8). It seemed like she was imploring them to hear the truth that sustained her.

I often wondered how she could smile when she seemed so alone. Few people ever stopped to acknowledge her words, and I never saw anyone visit her. Her apparent contentment with her daily existence often puzzled me.

One day, as I passed her on my way out and she declared the familiar words of God's goodness, the reason for her contentment struck me as if God had spoken audibly to me. When her mental capacities and reasoning abilities had faded, what remained were the words of praise for her Lord that now overflowed from the depths of her heart.

It occurred to me that God knew her place there and how her words would encourage me (and many others who passed her in the hallway). The praise that must have carried her through many trials was now God's provision to sustain me in mine. Her life had been long, and her remaining days on earth would be few, yet she was able to praise God and bring glory to His name.

From that day forward, whenever I passed her, I thought, *Thank you, Lord, for placing this precious woman in this home. May I be used by You until my dying day to bring sweet adoration and praise to Your name.*

—Jan Peterson

Embracing God's Truth

Jan struggled with many emotions as she visited her father in a nursing home. God knew Jan's struggles and positioned in her path a woman whose praise and adoration for Him served to encourage and sustain Jan through that difficult time.

God is present in an atmosphere of praise. Psalm 22:3 (KJV) says, "Thou art holy, O thou that inhabitest the praises of Israel."

After King Solomon completed construction of the temple, he called all the people of Israel to gather as the ark of the covenant, a sacred chest, was placed in the most holy place in the temple. It was over this chest that the Spirit of God dwelled. When the ark had been set in place, the priests who had carried it withdrew from the holy place in anticipation of God's Spirit descending to fill it.

Read 2 Chronicles 5:12–14. According to verses 13–14, what happened as the people began to sing and praise God? ______________________________

____

____

____

____

As the people praised God, His Spirit descended and the glory of the Lord filled the temple with such power that the priests could not perform their service. When we choose to praise God, we usher His Spirit into our circumstances.

The elderly, wheelchair-bound woman at the nursing home must have chosen, when her mind was young and strong, to praise God often in order for those words and sentiments to remain embedded deep within her heart. For even in her frailty, whenever she opened her lips, her mouth was compelled to praise the God she loved.

Read Isaiah 46:4. What does God tell His people He will do for them, even in their old age? ____

____

____

____

____

Even when our bodies are old and our hair has faded to gray, our Lord will sustain us. He is unchanging and ever worthy of our praise.

Read Psalm 150 out loud. Then write your own psalm of personal praise to God for the things He has done in your life. ________________________

____

____

____

____

Chapter Seventeen

Compassionate Intervention

The LORD is gracious and compassionate,
slow to anger and rich in love.

Psalm 145:8

As I watched a group of people standing outside, holding signs, and shouting at women as they approached the clinic where abortions were performed, my heart was overwhelmed with compassion for those women who were wrestling with that choice.

I tried to imagine their feelings as they entered the clinic. I couldn't believe that the decision to abort could be made coldly, without emotion. Faced with an unexpected pregnancy, women feel trapped and afraid, unsure where to turn. I wondered what impact the protesters had on their decisions.

It all seemed overwhelming to me. Surely, I thought, there must be a more compassionate way to encourage women to choose life. I knew there had to be a different approach to the problem of unwanted pregnancies, but I wasn't aware of any organization that offered the help I thought was necessary.

One Sunday I saw a display at my church that included brochures from a pregnancy crisis center. I picked one up, intending to read through it, but set it aside after I got home. I saw the brochures each week as I entered the church. *I don't want to be involved with an organization that isn't compassionate toward women,* I thought as I walked by the display, trying to ignore the tug in my heart. Finally, reluctantly, I contacted the center. They offered a volunteer training class. I decided to give it a try, but I vowed to bow out the moment I sensed a spirit of condemnation toward the women they were there to serve.

At the first training session, the director said, "We're the kinder, gentler side of pro-life." Her words helped me relax. She also helped me understand that not everyone who stands outside an abortion clinic is there to condemn. Some offer alternatives in a caring way, just as I wanted to do. After completing the course, I became a volunteer peer counselor, and my life was changed forever.

As a volunteer I spent four hours each week visiting with young women who came to the center for free pregnancy tests. I interviewed them to determine their needs—materially, emotionally, and spiritually. I listened without judgment as they described their circumstances. I set a personal goal of befriending one woman and walking her through her pregnancy, providing support and compassion all along the way. I had no idea that I'd spend several years volunteering at the clinic, becoming involved in the lives of many women with unplanned pregnancies.

I now serve as the center's executive director. I work with a staff of women committed to showing compassion toward women in crisis pregnancies. We don't judge them. We reach out to them and tell them about the love and acceptance they can find in Jesus. As I reflect on the many women we've ministered to at the center, I find great peace and joy in the small role I have played in a kind and gentle pro-life organization. I believe it is the approach Jesus would take.

—Mona Parish

Embracing God's Truth

Mona was deeply concerned about the women who felt compelled to have abortions. Protesting seemed to address only the decision, not the women making it. When she volunteered at a pregnancy center, she discovered a compassionate and loving approach to crisis pregnancies that not only affected the women's decisions with regard to their babies but also often changed the course of their lives.

Compassion is expressed when we take action that helps alleviate someone's suffering. One day some religious leaders brought a woman who had been caught committing adultery to see Jesus. Read John 8:1–11.

Jesus was teaching in the temple courts, surrounded by a crowd of people, when the Pharisees and the teachers of the Law marched in, dragging the woman with them. They forced her to stand (probably half-dressed) in front of everyone while they publicly announced her sin.

How would you feel if you were brought before your church congregation and the leaders publicly listed your recent sins? ____________________

____

____

____

____

What was the motive behind the religious leaders' actions (verse 6)?

____

____

____

____

These men weren't truly interested in justice, and Jesus knew it. They were using this woman—humiliating her in front of everyone—in an effort to trap Jesus into contradicting the Law so they could arrest Him.

Jesus simply ignored their question and began to write in the sand. When the timing was right, He stood up, looked at the men, and urged the one standing among them who was without sin to throw the first stone. Then He bent down and continued writing in the sand as the woman braced herself for the first blow.

I imagine tears flowed down her cheeks as, one by one, the men walked away. According to the Law she deserved to be stoned. Yet what was Jesus' response to the woman in verses 10–11? ______________________________

____

____

____

____

He didn't overlook her sin, but Jesus lovingly urged her to live differently from then on. He was compassionate toward those suffering around Him, perhaps because His mission was to suffer and die so that we can live differently for all eternity.

Ask God to provide opportunities to intervene compassionately when confronted with the mistakes and suffering of people around you. It's the approach Jesus would take.

Chapter Eighteen

The Heavenly Pillowmaker

Brothers, we do not want you to . . .
grieve like the rest of men,
who have no hope.

1 Thessalonians 4:13

I was sitting at the kitchen table one September morning, eating a peach and enjoying the sunshine's warmth as it streamed through our skylight, when the phone rang. When I answered, I was greeted by a pleasant female voice that asked, "Are you a relative of Meredith Fletcher?"

"Yes, I'm her mother," I responded cheerfully, assuming it was the college with another question. Our daughter Meredith was scheduled to begin her freshman year the next day. I smiled as I pictured my beautiful eighteen-year-old, five-foot two-inch, blond-haired daughter.

"Meredith has been in a serious car accident," the woman said. "You need to speak to the doctor."

Panic overtook me. "Oh, God, help me," I cried out.

In my head I could hear my daughter's oft-given advice: "Mom, don't overreact! Everything will be okay." Remembering her words helped me remain calm while I waited for the doctor to come to the phone. When he finally did, he asked, "Do you have anyone there with you?"

"No, but you've got to tell me," I demanded. I knew my nursing background would enable me to understand any injury the doctor described.

Quietly, he said, "Meredith has been in a serious car accident, and she has passed away."

Passed away?! I thought. How could Meredith be dead when she was so alive?

"I need to give you my phone number," the doctor continued. "Call back for the details when you have someone with you."

I immediately phoned my husband at work. He called the doctor and learned that Meredith had been in the backseat, behind the driver, in a friend's car. The car was hit broadside by a tractor-trailer, killing both Meredith and the boy at the wheel instantly.

When my husband got home, we left for Walla Walla, Washington, where both Meredith and our older daughter, Madelyn, had been living. After the seven-hour drive, we joined Madelyn and stood by Meredith's body. Her head rested on a pillow. I ran my fingers through her hair. The cuts on her pretty face looked like they could easily heal. She appeared to be sleeping, but her skin felt strangely cold. I longed for Jesus to walk into the room and wake her up.

That night I reassured myself that God had been with her. But I couldn't understand why He hadn't prevented her death. The next morning we visited the two girls who had survived the accident. They told us that the boy driving had prayed before they left the campus. The knowledge that God had been especially invited to be with her in the car was comforting.

Later that day Madelyn talked about the last month she had lived with her sister, sharing work, play, music, and secrets. Two days before Meredith had moved into the dorm, her last words to her sister were "I'll see you in the morning."

After three days of handling details, we drove home. The mortuary transported Meredith, and we began to make plans immediately.

"I've never planned a funeral," I confessed to the funeral director.

He was a fellow church member who knew and loved Meredith. He encouraged us to think about how she would have planned it. We'd often discussed plans for the wedding she would have someday, but we'd never talked about her funeral. Madelyn remembered Meredith telling a friend, "If you ever have a funeral for me, make it light, cheerful, and casual."

I felt upheld on a pillow of memories as we talked about her favorite songs, her favorite Bible chapter, and her preferences in life. Organ music didn't reflect Meredith's personality, so her favorite Steve Green music was played as guests joined our family in the bittersweet celebration of our daughter's short but full life. When the service ended, we were ushered out by a powerful song that encouraged everyone to remember that Jesus has conquered death.

I'd been journaling my prayers for years, and this tragedy intensified my desire to record every thought, need, and heartfelt prayer. Later, reviewing my entries during the time following my daughter's death, I was blessed by the many ways God comforted me.

One day I wrote, "Thank You, Father, for giving us the ideas for a funeral, helping us to choose a casket, and guiding us to find a cemetery that was as right for her as such awful things can be." Later I wrote, "Thank You for her favorite song that played on the radio, for the church member who offered to take me to the store, and for the grief book that was marked in the exact spot with the answer I needed today."

I phoned our pastor's wife and shared the many blessings I'd noted in my prayer journal. She called the blessings "God's pillows to cushion the blow." The many pillows from God gave us the strength to cope. The softest pillow of all—the one we've fallen back on numerous times throughout the years—is the hope of resurrection.

We cling to the promise of the great Pillowmaker: "The last enemy to be destroyed is death. . . . For the trumpet will sound, the dead will be raised imperishable" (1 Corinthians 15:26, 52). Our family looks forward to the day when Madelyn can finally have Meredith's final words fulfilled: "I'll see you in the morning."

—Lana Fletcher

Embracing God's Truth

The inexpressible pain of losing Meredith was cushioned by the evidence of God's activity in the midst of the Fletcher family's grief. God's comforting presence enabled Lana and her family to focus their thoughts heavenward, to the day they will see their beloved Meredith again.

Believers in Jesus Christ do not have to grieve without hope. Read 1 Thessalonians 4:13–18. What encouragement do you find in verse 17?

____

____

We will attend a glorious heavenly reunion when Jesus returns! Can you just imagine the celebration as we meet our Lord and see loved ones from years past?

Are there any loved ones whom you look forward to seeing again in heaven? If so, who? ____

____

____

It's natural to grieve when someone close to us dies. But in the midst of our pain, we can find encouragement and strength as we look forward to the day when all believers in Christ will be together again—living forever in the presence of our Lord.

Chapter Nineteen

Singing over Broken Nails

He will take great delight in you,
he will quiet you with his love,
he will rejoice over you with singing.

Zephaniah 3:17

It was 6:47 A.M., and I sat at my desk with unwashed hair, wearing a pair of comfy pajamas with a ripped hem on one side. My toenail was broken and covered with a Band-Aid. I longed for an iced cinnamon Danish rather than the egg white, wheat toast, and skim milk before me. The children were still sleeping, and I was enjoying every second of peace to myself with my morning cup of coffee.

I surveyed my quiet house. The toilets needed cleaning, and the laundry was piled in front of the washer. I had a stack of notes, ideas, devotional guides, and women's magazines on my kitchen counter. A thin layer of dust coated the furniture. The garbage needed to be taken out, and toy army camps were scattered, destroyed and abandoned, in my living room.

Any Clean Queen would have recommended I tackle these messes the night before so that I could rise with clean thoughts and a clean spirit and be ready for a bright, new day. But with three little ones in my house, I'd spent my evening wrestling them into pajamas, wielding toothbrushes, stepping on fire trucks on the way to bunk beds, and snatching dirty clothes off the floor before stealing a few sweet kisses at prayer time. I remember letting out a sigh as I closed the last bedroom door.

Feelings of failure and unworthiness welled up within me as I blended hazelnut creamer into my coffee. But I sensed God whispering Zephaniah 3:17 to my spirit, a verse that I've highlighted in my Bible. He reminded me that He loves me even before my house is clean; before I've showered, put on makeup, covered my broken toenail, and put on clothes without Popsicle stains.

From the beginning of time, women have had countless chores to do. Many of us have a few pounds to lose, both in flesh and attitude. We all battle against endless dust and cluttered homes, and eventually we get gray hair. But despite all our flaws, our Lord takes great delight in us. When we seek Him, He will quiet us with His love. Even when we have dirty toilets and broken toenails, our God rejoices over each of us with singing.

—Cyndy Gusler

Embracing God's Truth

Cyndy allowed her perceived shortcomings to make her feel unworthy of God's love. But He sweetly reminded her of a passage from His Word that reassured her of His love for her.

According to Romans 5:7–8, how do we know that God's love is not based on our worthiness?____

Read Romans 8:1–3. What assurances do we have as believers in Jesus Christ?____

What further encouragement do you gain from Romans 8:38–39?

The next time feelings of failure and unworthiness well up in your heart, remember that nothing can separate you from God's love.

Read Zephaniah 3:14–17 and note the reasons Israel was told to rejoice.

____

____

____

____

____

Through Jesus, our sins have been taken away. He is with us (Matthew 1:23), and through Him we never again have to fear condemnation, for our King is mighty to save. Consider highlighting these passages in your Bible, as Cyndy did. Be glad and rejoice! For God takes great delight in you and rejoices over you with singing.

Chapter Twenty

Mother of the Groom

Let us hold unswervingly to the hope we profess, for he who promised is faithful.

Hebrews 10:23

Walking down the country church aisle, I carried the groom's candle toward its designated position next to the unity candle. I couldn't believe that my youngest son, Kevin, was getting married and I was being honored as mother of the groom. As I slowly made my way toward the front, memories flooded my mind. I remembered the day I discovered I was pregnant; the first time I looked into Kevin's tiny face; his first tooth, first wobbly step, first day of school . . . But the first chapter of memories passed quickly, as had the days with my son.

My divorce had been as amiable as one can be. I understood when custody was awarded to my ex-husband: after all, Kevin was almost twelve, and I have multiple sclerosis. But we lived in the same town, and I had every expectation of being involved in my son's life. Little did I know that it would be many years before I would see or even hear from Kevin. I returned from a short trip with friends to discover that Kevin and his dad had moved away without leaving a forwarding address.

As I continued down the long aisle, the second chapter of my memories began to unfold. My heartache resurfaced as I recalled the long, silent years following Kevin's move. No one in my family had heard from him. I spent many nights crying out to God, praying for my son and for some sort of contact with him. Woven into that second painful chapter of memories was a promise, spoken to my heart by God through His Word: "Do not be afraid, for I am with you; I will bring your children from the east and gather you from the west" (Isaiah 43:5). That promise was the anchor to which I desperately clung for years.

Six years after my last conversation with Kevin, I stepped into a classroom where I was scheduled to teach Sunday school. A friend turned to me and asked, "Chris, do you have a son?"

Stunned, I turned and said, "You know something. What is it?"

"We have some temporary help at work for a couple weeks. One of the boys used to live here and is looking for his mother. Do you know Kevin?"

I slumped to the floor in disbelief. My son was just fifteen minutes away and wanted to find me! I immediately assumed God was answering all my prayers and fulfilling the promise He'd so clearly spoken to my heart.

The next morning I, along with two friends, headed to the restaurant where Kevin was working. After we talked to the manager, one of my friends went inside to talk to Kevin. He wouldn't come out to see me but said he would call later. That call never came. For whatever reason, Kevin chose not to contact me. I tried to call him several times, but my calls were never returned.

My mind was reeling. Why didn't he want to talk to me? Did he blame me for the divorce? Did he think I hadn't wanted custody of him? I had so many questions and no answers. Kevin soon left town, and I was left confused, still clinging to God's promise.

Five more years crept by without any contact from Kevin. Then one day I received a phone call from my daughter. She had heard from Kevin. She informed me that he was getting married, and I was invited to the wedding. Thirty minutes later I was talking to my son.

Now, as I set the groom's candle in place, I realized that God had kept His promise and also answered my constant prayer for a godly influence to enter Kevin's life. Kevin stood tall and proud, waiting for his bride, who was clearly the godly influence for which I had prayed so earnestly. He was starting a new chapter in his life, and we were starting a new chapter in our relationship. It began with a long walk down a country church aisle, being honored as mother of the groom.

—Christine Callaway-Crowley

Embracing God's Truth

After being separated from her son for eleven years, Christine's mind flooded with memories as she attended his wedding and recognized God's faithfulness to reunite her with her son and allow her to be honored as mother of the groom.

God is compassionate toward those who experience the loss of a loved one, even when He knows they will be reunited in the future.

Read John 11:1–6.

God didn't reunite Christine with her son for eleven years. Jesus intentionally waited days before responding to Mary and Martha's plea to help Lazarus. Have you ever felt that God didn't respond quickly enough during a crisis in your life? If so, describe your feelings at that time. ____________________

____

____

How does verse 5 encourage you? ____________________________

____

____

____

____

Read John 11:17–32. What did Martha and Mary say to Jesus when He finally arrived in Bethany (verses 21 and 32)? ____________________________

____

____

____

____

Read John 11:33. Jesus knew He was about to resurrect Lazarus. He didn't cry over his death. He was deeply troubled and wept when He saw the pain the people were experiencing as a result of their loss. What do you find comforting about Jesus's response to their grief? ____________________________

____

____

____

____

Read John 11:34–44. The next time you experience pain over the loss of a loved one, be assured that Jesus is moved by your pain. And whether you are reunited in this life or you have to wait for the reunion of all believers in heaven, you can look forward to the day when the bride of Christ (Ephesians 5:25–27) will be gathered together and honored at the blessed wedding supper in heaven (Revelation 19:6–9).

Chapter Twenty-one

An Unexpected Ministry

Not that we are competent in ourselves to claim anything for ourselves, but our competence comes from God.

2 Corinthians 3:5

I attended church most of my life, but my focus was on me—my wants, my desires, my needs. A weekend ladies retreat changed everything.

The retreat began on Friday evening with a speaker whose entire talk was about prayer. I was bored out of my mind. The next morning the speaker again talked about prayer . . . prayer . . . prayer. After what seemed like an eternity, she dismissed us with instructions to find a quiet place away from everyone to pray (of course) for about an hour using a handout she'd prepared. Wonderful, I thought to myself, I'll take my quilt and my pillow and take a good nap. But God had other plans.

As I prepared for my snooze, I glanced at the speaker's handout.

Revelation 3:15–16 caught my attention. "I know your deeds, that you are neither cold nor hot. I wish you were either one or the other! So, because you are lukewarm—neither hot nor cold—I am about to spit you out of my mouth." I didn't remember ever hearing that verse.

The next scripture on the page was John 3:16. "God so loved the world that he gave his one and only Son, that whoever believes in him shall not perish but have eternal life." As I read that passage, the reality of God's sacrifice on my behalf became real to me for the first time.

Before the hour ended, I'd made a promise to God that I would pray and read my Bible every day. Although it was difficult at first, I kept my promise, and over the next few months Scripture came to life for me. I sensed God's presence when I prayed and I was able to recognize when He was speaking to me.

One day I read an article about a Brazilian woman's God-given burden for the vast number of her country's young people whose lives were being destroyed by immorality, alcoholism, and drug abuse. She and her husband held a meeting for mothers to pray for their children. Amazingly, the article stated that more than six hundred mothers attended that first prayer meeting.

The article was at the forefront of my mind for the next week. I kept thinking we should do something similar at my church. I shared the information with my pastor and told him that I thought we should have a day of prayer for mothers in our church. He loved the idea and suggested I call it "Mom's Day of Prayer."

Just two years earlier I had been living as though God didn't exist. I certainly didn't feel worthy to organize a Mom's Day of Prayer. But as I prayed and clung to my recently developed trust in God, I sensed that we should not only do it but also open the event to women throughout our community. I contacted my pastor again. He wholeheartedly agreed and quoted Isaiah 56:7: "My house will be called a house of prayer for all nations." He ended the conversation by praying for the first Mom's Day of Prayer and all those to be held in the future. I chuckled at his enthusiasm, but I began making preparations.

A friend suggested I select a Bible verse for the event. I agreed, but my knowledge of Scripture was minimal. As I thought back over the stories I'd heard in Sunday school, I couldn't remember a single instance in which a mother prayed for her child.

A few days later I ran into our church's youth minister and asked him if he had any ideas for a verse we could use for the Mom's Day of Prayer. He told me he'd give it some thought. I was surprised when he called me about three hours later and read from 1 Samuel 1:27–28. "I prayed for this child, and the LORD has granted me what I asked of him. So now I give him to the LORD. For his whole life he will be given over to the LORD." The youth minister said, "That's Hannah's prayer for her son Samuel." Overwhelmed, I quickly thanked him and hung up the phone. Tears streamed down my face as I grabbed my Bible and read about Hannah. I sobbed as I realized that God had used the youth minister to lead me to just the right verse.

Mom's Day of Prayer, shortened to MDOP, is now a worldwide movement. 1 Samuel 1:27–28 appears on all of the MDOP materials and on our Web site. God has been with me as I've taken each step necessary to expand the MDOP ministry. By His grace, Mom's Day of Prayer is changing many hearts and lives . . . the first of which was mine.

—*Kathy Coleman*

Embracing God's Truth

Kathy was just an ordinary woman whom God used to accomplish an extraordinary task. Nothing in her background suggested that she would become the founder of a worldwide prayer movement. Kathy simply sought God and made herself available for whatever He wanted to do through her life.

Read 1 Corinthians 1:26–31 and note why God might choose unlikely people to accomplish some of His greatest work. ______________________

____

____

____

____

Have you ever felt unworthy or inadequate to serve in your church or in a ministry? If so, describe the circumstances. ____________________

____

____

____

____

How does Kathy's story encourage you? ____________________

____

____

____

____

2 Corinthians 3:5 tells us that our competence comes from God. Ask God to show you how you can participate in His work. Be surrendered and ready. He just may use you to accomplish a great work.

Chapter Twenty-two

Moving Forward

Jesus said to his disciples, "If anyone would come after me, he must deny himself and take up his cross and follow me."

Matthew 16:24

We'd been in our new home for a full day. Moving from a small, rural community back to a larger city meant heftier taxes and higher house prices. God had clearly led my husband to a new job, but I felt like an uncooperative child being dragged along. My heart yearned to return to the house we'd built atop twelve acres of wooded land. The valley below offered a panorama of cows, trees, deer, wild turkey, and lush green. Just sitting on the porch, soaking in a sunset or stargazing, had been rejuvenating.

Our son, Ryan, had just graduated from high school, and our plan was for him to live at the house until it sold. We also left our two cats and the dog with him until we were able to get settled.

As I took a rest from my halfhearted attempt at unpacking in the new place, I poured my fears, doubts, misgivings, and questions onto the pages of my prayer journal. Finally spent, and knowing God wanted me to trust Him, I surrendered my unenthusiastic will. I wrote, "I guess I just need time to adjust . . . but Lord, help me trust in You!"

One hour later, the phone rang. It was my former neighbor. "Denise, your house is on fire! Honey [the dog] got out, but we don't know about the cats, and we're trying to track down Ryan. I'll call you back when we find him."

I hung up and fought the temptation to panic. Words to a song we'd sung at a recent women's retreat came to mind. "Where He leads me, I will follow," I said to myself.

Just then it seemed as though God whispered to my heart, "Did you mean that?"

With a sigh, I whispered back, "Yes, okay, Lord."

His calming peace was immediate, filling me with His strength. I called my husband, Ted, at the office, relayed the message about the fire, and then packed a small bag for the trek back to our old home.

It was late when we arrived. The air was thick with smoke, and Ryan was surrounded by a few friends from school. Sadly, the cats had both perished. The firemen kindly put their remains in pillowcases. Our dog was in shock but glad to see us. Best of all, Ryan was safe. Though it was too dark to see anything, we walked up our steep driveway. Everything looked lonely, bleak, and desolate. We surveyed what we could, but there was nothing more to be done. As we left the blackened scene, Ryan told us that he'd felt an impulse to leave the house that afternoon instead of taking a nap, as had been his intention.

The next morning we returned to the house. It looked worse by daylight. Our home was nothing but a charred, water-damaged skeleton. Ryan's entire room and all of his belongings had been destroyed. Had he stayed home napping, he, too, would have been a victim of the fire's ferocity. Tears of grief and thankfulness accompanied the burial of our two sweet cats, and when we finished, we quietly drove away from what had been our dream home one last time.

Shortly thereafter the property, with its sewer, well, and the house's foundation still intact, sold. The insurance money for the loss came quickly, allowing us to settle into our new home debt-free. Everything fell into place. It was as if God were telling us, "The past is behind. You can't go back. Keep moving forward."

So we will. Because the God we love and serve is faithful! I can say with renewed confidence, "Where He leads me, I will follow!"

—Denise Meagher

Embracing God's Truth

Denise was struggling to follow God's lead and leave behind a house and community she'd grown to love. When the house she'd treasured was destroyed by a fire within a day of moving into the new one, Denise recognized God's protection and accepted His obvious change of direction for her family.

How about you? Can you honestly say that you will follow wherever God leads you? If most of us were honest, we'd have to admit that there are some changes we'd struggle to embrace, just as Denise did. But if we truly want to follow and serve God, we must be willing to relinquish our will and accept His.

Read Matthew 16:21–22. What was Peter refusing to accept? ____________

____

____

____

How did Jesus respond in Matthew 16:23? ______________________

____

____

____

According to Mark 10:45, what was the reason Jesus came to Earth? ______

____

____

____

Peter was trying to interfere with God's plan and purpose for Jesus. Peter loved Jesus, but it was his selfish desire to have Jesus with him that spurred his passionate response.

Read Matthew 16:24. What did Jesus say we need to do if we want to follow Him?____

____

____

____

The deepest part of our inner being wants to have its own way. Peter was acting out of selfishness, not loyalty. What selfish desires do you struggle most to deny yourself?____

____

____

____

Denying ourselves takes a willful act of surrender. Sometimes, as with Denise and her move, we act like selfish children being dragged along when God leads us down a new path. But we need to learn to deny ourselves and surrender the need to have our own way if we ever truly want to be able to say, "Where He leads me, I will follow."

Chapter Twenty-three

Choosing Love

Love never fails.

1 Corinthians 13:8

"Will I ever have a positive relationship with my daughter?" I wondered aloud, not for the first time.

"Wait until she's twenty-one," a friend advised. "Everything will change then."

Twenty-one?! I thought. *I want to enjoy my daughter now.* But as Susan struggled with life as a teenager, a close relationship with her seemed impossible. We couldn't agree on anything, and with Susan fighting relentlessly for her independence, we argued about everything. Like the sunny flower known as black-eyed Susan, my Susan had always brightened our home. But in her teen years, Susan's dark eyes flashed daggers that could pierce the soul. What happened to my darling little girl? Oh, Lord, I want her back! I don't even think she likes me, and I'm not sure I like her, either.

"Loving and liking are not the same, Karen," I felt God whisper to my heart. I knew I needed to act lovingly regardless of how she responded. I wanted to see her through God's eyes. But each time I faced another confrontation with Susan, I had to consciously choose to love—and it was easier said than done.

When I asked God to let His love cover my inadequacy, without fail, He did. Still, clashes were frequent. Sometimes it was clear that we needed to put some space between us. More than once, either by her choice or mine and my husband's, Susan spent time living with another family until she was ready to come back home.

Our family moved from Florida to Michigan when Susan was a senior in high school. The timing of the move was difficult for her. But somehow Susan sensed that my despondency over the move was stronger than hers, and I began to sense her empathy. Cracks were showing in my veneer of self-sufficiency, revealing a vulnerability Susan hadn't previously recognized. The love I'd chosen to express toward her began to be reciprocated again. A friendship emerged, and we actually found ourselves looking forward to spending time together.

Adjusting to her new surroundings, Susan began to make new friends. One in particular became that special person with whom she would choose to spend the rest of her life.

One afternoon, as plans were being made for the wedding, I felt overwhelmed at the prospect of her leaving. I thought, *This is happening much too quickly and far too soon for me. Susan and I have just begun to enjoy each other's company, making up for lost time. I'm not ready to give her up to someone else.* As Susan continued talking about her wedding plans, I attempted to put my thoughts aside and concentrate on what she was saying. I tuned back in just in time to hear, "Mom, I want you to be my matron of honor—you're the best friend I have."

—Karen Kilby

Embracing God's Truth

Karen wondered if she would ever have a good relationship with her daughter, but as she relied on God to help her patiently love Susan unconditionally, the once strong relationship between them was eventually renewed.

You may not be dealing with a hormonal teenager, but we all have family members we find difficult to love.

The Greek word often used for love is agape. Agape is the kind of love God feels for us as His children. It is an unconditional, godly kind of love. The only way we can display agape love for others is through the power of the Holy Spirit living within us.

Read 1 Corinthians 13:1–3. What do you learn about the importance of love in the life of a believer?____________________________

____

____

____

____

Choosing to love is the "most excellent way" to live (1 Corinthians 12:31). We tend to assume that people displaying outward signs of being God-followers are "spiritual," but God cares far more about the heart—the attitude with which we do our works. And we may face no greater test of our hearts than family relationships. Unfortunately, sometimes we act the least lovingly toward the people closest to us.

Read 1 Corinthians 13:4–7 and list the attributes it says will be present in a heart filled with agape love.____________________________

____

____

____

____

With which aspects of agape love do you most often struggle when dealing with your family members? ______________________________________

____

____

____

Write a prayer asking God to empower you to overcome any envy, pride, or selfishness that interferes with your ability to truly love your family members as God loves you. ______________________________________

____

____

____

As Karen struggled to be patient and kind regardless of her daughter's behavior, she wisely sought God's help to act lovingly toward her daughter. It can be difficult for a parent to display agape love when dealing with the dramatic, self-centered behavior that is typical of teenagers. But what command did Jesus give us in John 13:34? ______________________________________

____

____

____

Rely upon God's power as you choose to respond to your family with agape love. Lean on Him for the strength to persevere through difficult times in your relationships. We are commanded to love. When we choose to always protect, always trust, always hope, and always persevere, we'll discover, as Karen did, that agape love never fails.

Chapter Twenty-four

Steps of Faith

Peter got down out of the boat,
walked on the water and
came toward Jesus.

Matthew 14:29

I was the oldest of five children when my mother tragically passed away from a liver ailment. With five children under the age of nine to care for on his own, my father was encouraged by relatives and friends to put us into an orphanage. But he was a man of great faith, and he trusted God to provide and keep our family together. Five years after my mother's death, my father married a young woman who not only became a dedicated wife but also created a loving and nurturing environment for our entire family. It was clear to me from an early age that God had taken care of us. His faithful provision and my father's strong faith fostered in me a strong desire to serve and honor Him in a special way.

After graduating from high school, I sensed God calling me to spend my life serving Him in a full-time vocation. After much prayer, I answered that call by becoming Sister Mary Mark of The Sisters of St. Benedict of Ferdinand, Indiana. In that Benedictine community, God has graciously blessed me and given me the opportunity to help many children. I served as a first-grade teacher for twelve years. While I enjoyed teaching, God developed an even greater passion in my heart for children with needs that couldn't be met in a standard classroom.

It was while I was working on my master's degree in special education that God first brought a child with special needs to our school. It became clear that the boy needed more than our programs and experience could provide, and the other nuns in my community asked if I would consider starting a special school. I didn't have a lot of experience with special education, and the idea was intimidating. But as I prayed about the prospect of taking on such a task, God directed me to the story about Jesus walking on water.

Jesus' disciples watched in fear and wonder as He walked across the water toward them. But He urged them not to be afraid. As I read Peter's response, I felt God speaking to me. "'Lord, if it's you,' Peter replied, 'tell me to come to you on the water.' 'Come,' he [Jesus] said. Then Peter got down out of the boat, walked on the water and came toward Jesus. But when he saw the wind, he was afraid and, beginning to sink, cried out, 'Lord, save me!' Immediately Jesus reached out his hand and caught him. 'You of little faith,' he said, 'why did you doubt?'"(Matthew 14:28–31).

As God spoke to my spirit, He gave me the faith to step out of my safe, secure boat. With prayer, the support of my community, and the guidance of the Holy Spirit, I was able to organize and open the Marian Day School in Evansville, Indiana. Many students' lives have been enriched. Children who were unable to speak when they came to the school learned to talk and even read because of the loving care and speech therapy we provided. Our work changed many lives.

After eleven successful years, God again began to nudge me out of my boat of familiarity and comfort. Our community became aware of a group of parents in Memphis, Tennessee, who were searching for a school for special children. With God's blessing and the prayers of all the Benedictine Sisters, I, along with two of my sisters, moved south to open another school in Memphis. Parents, friends, and neighbors worked hard to get Madonna Learning Center up and running.

Not long after we opened, a gentleman who had heard about the work we were doing for special-needs children left $35,000 to the school in his will. When we received the funds, the sisters in the community urged me to seek the counsel of a business manager, who suggested we set up an endowment fund—another uncomfortable step out onto the water with Jesus. Amazingly, many people believed in our work and contributed to the fund. Madonna Learning Center's building was miraculously paid off in one year.

It's impossible to say how many special students have been touched by the work at the schools through the years, but each one has a special place in my heart. I served as administrator at Madonna Learning Center for thirty-one years. It was a labor of love. Most of all, it was a labor of faith, walking step by step with my eyes fixed on Jesus.

—Sister Mary Mark Graf

Embracing God's Truth

As Sister Mary Mark kept her focus on Jesus, she often had to leave the security of familiar and comfortable situations. Because she chose to step out of her "boat," she experienced the joy of knowing that her steps were directed by the God who has the power to provide for the unique needs of every one of His children.

Read Matthew 14:22–26. As Jesus walked on the lake toward the boat, the disciples were terrified. Perhaps their sense of panic was intensified because they hadn't ever seen Jesus walk on water. Fear is often our first response when we're faced with unfamiliar or unexpected circumstances.

Are you facing any unfamiliar or unexpected situations right now? If so, what is your greatest fear? ____

____

____

____

Read Matthew 14:27–33. What caught Peter's attention and caused him to sink? ____

____

____

____

The fear that Peter had overcome for that brief walk on the water came flooding back. Whenever Jesus calls you to leave comfortable, secure surroundings, be prepared for the winds of uncertainty to challenge your faith.

What winds of uncertainty are challenging your faith at this time?

____

____

____

____

Fix your eyes on the Savior. He can calm even the strongest winds. Like Sister Mary Mark and the apostle Peter, you'll discover that even short walks on the water are far more rewarding than long rides in the same old boat.

Chapter Twenty-five

Saturday-Morning Sadness

Peace I leave with you; my peace I give you.

John 14:27

It was a warm summer Texas day. Our women's Bible study group was scheduled to begin the next week, and the leaders had gathered to prepare for the kickoff. After glad-to-see-you-again hugs, we all gathered for a time of prayer and praise. One woman after another began to sing the chorus of her favorite worship song. Sweet female voices harmonized as we all joined in. When it was my turn to lead, I began singing, "My Peace I Give unto You." Evidently I was the only one who knew the words, because I sang the entire chorus by myself. We all laughed about my unexpected solo as we began our planning session.

During the morning break, I was surprised to see the youngest of my three grown sons appear at the door. From the look on his face, I knew something was terribly wrong. He choked out the words, "Kevin's gone."

Kevin, my middle son, had been coming home from work when he was killed instantly in a car accident. My sweet son—a faithful husband with sons of his own, compassionate, fun-loving, and godly—was gone.

As I followed my youngest son home, I said, "God, this morning when I left home I had three sons." His response, spoken to my heart, was immediate: "You still do."

As the weeks following Kevin's death passed, I thought about how Jesus' disciples must have felt on the Saturday following His crucifixion. What a surreal time that must have been for them. I imagine they felt sadness, disappointment, confusion, and doubt, all mixed with the precious memories of their time with Him. They had traveled, eaten, and laughed together. They had watched Him love, heal, deliver, and teach. They had clung to His every word. Then, as the sun rose one Saturday morning, Jesus wasn't there.

I, too, had been catapulted into a Saturday-morning kind of sadness. The memories I had of Kevin were mixed with disappointment, pain, and confusion. But the disciples' Saturday-morning grief was followed by Sunday morning's joy. I have the advantage of knowing that Jesus didn't remain in that tomb. He overcame the ugly grasp of death, and His resurrection that Sunday morning not only transformed the lives of His disciples—it also transforms me.

Looking back, I recognize that my a cappella rendition of "My Peace I Give Unto You" was God's way of preparing me. I've learned that the peace that passes all understanding is most powerfully realized amid tremendous pain. Kevin is alive in heaven, and one day I will see him again. I choose to believe that Saturday is not the end. When Saturday-morning sadness begins to shadow me once again, I choose to remember Jesus. His resurrection serves as proof that Sunday morning is coming.

—Carol Rhodes

Embracing God's Truth

After suddenly losing her son, Carol found comfort and strength as she identified with the disciples' grief on the day following Jesus' death. The peace she found in the midst of her loss was based on her faith in Jesus Christ and her belief that she would one day see her son again in heaven.

Have you ever experienced the Saturday-morning sadness Carol described? If so, describe the circumstances. ______________________________

____

____

____

Read John 14:25–31. When Jesus reminded the disciples that He would be going away, He was preparing them for His impending death on the cross. What else did Jesus remind them would happen? ____________________

____

____

____

According to verse 29, what was the reason Jesus told His disciples ahead of time about His death and resurrection? ____________________________

____

____

____

When Jesus told His disciples of His death, He also said, "My peace I give unto you" (KJV)—the very words God whispered to Carol's heart that morning as she sang her solo of praise. What promise did Jesus make in John 14:1–3?

____

How is Jesus described in 1 Corinthians 15:20? ____________________

In Old Testament times, the first and best fruits of a harvest were presented to God as what was known as the firstfruits offering. Those fruits served as an example and a guarantee that the rest of the harvest was to come. Because Jesus was resurrected after His death, He serves as an example and a guarantee that believers who die will also overcome death. Jesus is the firstfruit of the harvest of souls. Because of Him, we can be assured that our Saturday-morning kind of sadness will one day be followed by a Sunday-morning type of joy as Jesus takes us all to the place He has prepared for us in heaven. That assurance can bring us peace—the kind of peace that only Jesus' resurrection can provide.

Chapter Twenty-six

Banged-Up Beauties

My grace is sufficient for you,
for my power is made perfect in weakness.

2 Corinthians 12:9

One day, as I looked in the mirror, I thought, *This isn't the same image that used to look back at me. Where was I when all of this happened?* Crow's-feet, little bags below my eyes, lines, and stretch marks were my latest fashion accessories. In a world obsessed with physical beauty, it seemed my beauty buggy was slipping down a snowy slope, careening down toward the valley of no return.

I know that beauty is not dependent on flawless skin and silky hair, but there is a place deep inside me that still struggles with the desire to go uphill rather than down. The bags under my eyes aren't the bags with which I'd prefer to accessorize.

Later that day my daughter, Stephanie, and I were running errands when we stumbled upon a garage sale. Our eyes were immediately drawn to a nightstand. It obviously had seen many years, and the dark solid mahogany was covered with several layers of white paint. The three small stacked drawers in the front screeched as we opened them and stuck as we tried to close them.

Upon closer inspection, we noticed that this little stand had once been attached to a larger unit. Apparently it had broken away from the original piece. It was old, musty, and pretty banged up. But as we studied its design and used our imaginations, we both agreed it had great potential. We paid full price, and the homeowner shook her head as we excitedly made our way to the car with our treasure.

When we arrived home, we set the dresser on the back porch for inspection. Initially, we circled the piece with a critical eye. We both agreed that it needed paint to cover its many flaws. We wondered if upkeep would be a burden, thinking it might need a fresh coat of paint each year. But as we stood there sizing up the little chest, sipping lemonade, and enjoying the springtime Oklahoma breeze, God began to speak to us.

We were viewing the dresser with the same perspective with which we had often examined ourselves: assuming beauty could only be achieved if all blemishes and imperfections were covered up. Yet each scratch and nick in the old banged-up bureau reflected its history—made it distinctive and unique. After a few moments of silence, Stephanie and I began to see what God sees in each of us: There is beauty in those blemishes.

With our new perspective, we traded our thoughts of paintbrushes for sandpaper as we aspired to uncover the unique beauty of the old piece. As we worked, our conversation centered on the many ways God can use our scars, pain, aging, and brokenness for His good purposes. We discussed how our weaknesses can make us more relatable to others and cause us to be more dependent on Him.

As the paint around the edges of the dresser came off, we agreed to allow our coverup to be peeled back as well. No longer would we try to conceal the parts of our personalities that others might consider quirky, or the pain of our past. Instead, we would begin sharing our flaws with other "bag" ladies. We committed to removing our masks of perfection, and we felt a surge of energy as we agreed to let others see us as we really are—banged-up beauties dearly loved by our Creator.

We all have been nicked and dented by life's journey. Rather than covering up our scars and imperfections, we need to allow God to sand off the superficial coverup and allow the world to see the flaws that make us distinctive and unique.

Now, whenever I feel the urge to try to reverse my body's downhill slide, I keep in mind that Jesus knows all about climbing uphill. He lovingly walked up the hill at Calvary to die on a cross because my soul's condition concerned Him far more than my physical condition.

When the apostle Paul asked God to remove a physical flaw that tormented him, God's response was, "My grace is sufficient for you, for my power is made perfect in weakness" (2 Corinthians 12:9). Yes, I am a banged-up beauty; but now I recognize that those "flaws" reflect my history—that the dents and scratches from living life are actually my greatest beauty secrets.

—Cyndi Schatzman

Embracing God's Truth

Cyndi was focusing on her imperfections with a critical eye. God changed her perspective by allowing her to see beauty in the flaws of an old banged-up bureau that she found at a garage sale. What physical aspects of your appearance make you feel unacceptable? ______________________________

____

____

____

____

____

God is the only one who can see you with true clarity. Read Psalm 139:1–18 and note everything these passages indicate that God knows about you.

___

___

Your Creator knows you completely. He knows your thoughts, your words, your actions, your weaknesses . . . and your potential. Nothing is hidden from Him.

Look again at God's response when the apostle Paul asked for a physical flaw to be removed (2 Corinthians 12:7–9). Regardless of what undesired "accessories" or blemishes you bear, God knows how to lovingly restore you so that your weaknesses reflect His power in your life. Under His gentle hand, your life-scars become evidence of wounds He's healed: your pain verification of your dependence upon Him; your aging body a reflection of your history with Him; your brokenness proof that His work in your life is not yet complete.

And some day, when your body eventually slides downhill to the valley of death, your bags will be exchanged for a new accessory—a crown of righteousness, which the Lord, the righteous Judge, will award to you on that day (2 Timothy 4:7–8).

Chapter Twenty-seven

Heavenly Care

In my desperation I prayed,
and the Lord listened.

Psalm 34:6 NLT

In a matter of moments our youngest son was whisked away into an ambulance. The emergency-room MRI revealed that what was originally thought to be a virus was actually a life-threatening brain tumor. We followed the ambulance for several hours through the darkness of night to a children's hospital. Nick was admitted, and surgery was scheduled for the following week.

A nurse started an IV, and my mother and I settled in to stay with Nick. During the night, a number of different nurses came into his room to draw blood. The vein began to collapse, and it soon became apparent that they would need to start a new IV. After many sticks with a needle and many tears from sweet Nick, the medical staff finally was able to find a vein. Relief flooded over us as Nick fell into a peaceful sleep for the first time in hours.

His rest was interrupted abruptly around midnight when a nurse burst into the room, turned on the bright lights, and began talking in a loud, abrasive voice. Her manner and tone frightened Nick. As she finished her tasks and turned to leave, she told us she would be back around four in the morning to draw more blood and that he might have to endure yet another new IV. Nick began to cry immediately. Mother and I looked at each other in disbelief. How could she be so inconsiderate? Words could not express the fear and anxiety that filled my mind.

When Nick quieted and Mom lay next to him in bed, I began reading my Bible aloud to her and praying silently that God would spare Nick the quickly approaching round of more needles. At around 3:30 a.m. I slipped out of the room and into the lobby to call a friend and ask her to pray for Nick.

With my back against a wall, I slowly slid down into a near-fetal position and began to cry as I told her of the night's events. We ended our call, but I was still sitting on the floor with my knees drawn to my chest when a nurse walked by.

"Are you okay?" she asked gently.

"No," I replied with a weak shake of my head and tears streaming down my face.

She crouched down on the floor in front of me, and I told her all that had happened. When I finished talking, she took my hands, prayed for me, and told me she was the charge nurse for the evening. She explained that she normally never left her floor, but that night she had felt a strong urge to get a snack. We both knew God had orchestrated our meeting in the lobby. Then she said, "I'll do Nick's blood work at four o'clock."

When she entered Nick's room early that morning, you could feel the peace and love of God come in with her. Before she began to draw blood, she whispered a prayer. Everything went smoothly, and she said, "Thank You, Jesus," and gently patted Nick's little arm. He never even woke up. God had answered my prayer to spare Nick another terrifying experience in a way I never could have imagined.

I often reflect on that night in the hospital when I struggle with fear and doubt. That nurse was like an angel sent from heaven in our time of need. Throughout the past five years of Nick's continued battle with brain cancer, God has continued to answer prayer and work in amazing ways. Little did I know that night in the hospital would be only the first of many times God would listen and respond to the desperate cries of this mother for her son.

—Tammy Nischan

Embracing God's Truth

Tammy cried out to God to help her son. As she sat against the wall in the hallway, crying a Christian nurse saw her and responded to both her and Nick's needs with such gentle care that the little boy never even woke up as she did the necessary blood work. Tammy recognized the nurse as God's answer to her prayers for her son.

A woman named Hagar knew similar anguish as she cried out to God for her son. She was the servant of Abraham and Sarah, and when the couple was unable to have children, Sarah arranged for Hagar to become a surrogate mother of sorts. She bore Abraham a son named Ishmael, but when Sarah had a child herself, Hagar and her son were forced to leave.

Read Genesis 21:11–17. Hagar placed Ishmael under a bush to protect him from the sun, walked a short distance away, and sobbed. According to verse 17, whom did God hear crying? ______________________________

____

____

____

____

____

Through her tears, Hagar must have been asking God to respond to the cries of her son. Her son's suffering was more than she could bear. Interestingly, when Hagar first discovered she was pregnant with Ishmael, she also had an encounter with God in the desert.

Read Genesis 16:7–14. Hagar knew the Lord as "the God who sees me." Perhaps she didn't realize that He is a God who sees everyone and everything. Maybe, as she sat there crying out to God, she was begging Him to see her son as He had seen her.

Is there a situation or need that you're struggling to believe God can see? If so, express it in the space below. ______________________________

____

____

____

____

Now read God's response to Hagar in Genesis 21:18–19.

Our Lord is not only a God who sees but also a God who hears—and a God who cares about His children. He knows our needs, and He is able to meet them.

How does Tammy's (or Hagar's) story encourage you? ________________

____

____

____

____

Nick's charge nurse in the hospital that day was just as surely God's divine provision for him as was the angel of God who led Hagar to the life-sustaining well for Ishmael. God sees, hears, and responds to the prayers of His people with heavenly care.

Chapter Twenty-eight

Friendly Reunion

If it is possible,
as far as it depends on you,
live at peace with everyone.

Romans 12:18

Have you ever had a friend who let you down or hurt you? Are you always the loyal, reliable friend you should be to others? A close friend and I parted ways several years ago, and neither of us was without fault. With many long-standing issues, the relationship seemed broken beyond repair. I was sad and hurt—as was she. We both moved on with our lives, but we also continued to grieve the loss of our friendship. As time passed, we each made a few attempts to reconcile, but our efforts seemed futile. I finally surmised that the relationship simply wasn't meant to be.

I tried to put the friendship out of my mind and move on, but I couldn't. I loved my former friend deeply, and as much as I tried to convince myself (and others) that it didn't matter, it did. After three years of distance, I prayed and mustered up the courage to reach out to my long-lost friend through e-mail. I wrote:

> *I'm sorry. I love you. I miss knowing you. I desire to be real with you again. I don't want hurt feelings on either side, and I know there are. Will you forgive me for the things I've done to cause you pain?*

I waited nervously for her reply. We hadn't been good at communicating by e-mail. It seemed the written words, without the accompanying tone and facial expressions, had often added to our misunderstandings rather than clearing them up. I didn't even know if she was open to reconciliation, but I missed her enough to risk rejection by trying to reconnect.

Those years of separation from my friend caused me to draw closer to God. In the process I realized that my inability to reconcile with her had more to do with my fear of being vulnerable than with the many reasons we'd given for parting ways. I'd been more willing to walk away from the friendship than to be susceptible to more heartache. Reaching out was difficult for me. Asking for forgiveness was even more challenging. But I'd come to realize that both were necessary in my own healing process, regardless of the response to my plea.

A few days later I received a reply. To my great surprise, my old friend was open, willing, and ready to reconcile. She had also experienced growth in her relationship with God. We were now willing to humble ourselves and put the past behind us. It took both time and effort, but our friendship has been restored, and a new, genuine spirit of love and trust has developed between us. Our friendship stands as a constant reminder of what God can do when we make ourselves vulnerable first with Him, and then with others.

—Lisa Whittle

Embracing God's Truth

After the loss of a friendship, Lisa experienced spiritual growth that led her to a greater level of transparency with God. As a result, she was able to humble herself, ask for forgiveness, and be more vulnerable with her former friend. The result was a restored relationship.

Jacob and Esau were twin brothers who lived in constant conflict from the time they were in their mother's womb. Read Genesis 25:21–34 and note what you learn about each of these brothers.

Esau ____

____

____

Jacob ____

____

____

Esau was named for his hairy appearance. Jacob means "he grasps the heel" or, figuratively, "he deceives." They were polar opposites. Esau was a man's man, but Jacob could probably best be described as a mama's boy. Before the twins were even born, God told their mother, Rebekah, that the older would serve the younger.

What did Esau sell to Jacob (verse 33)? ____________________________

____

____

Esau was the firstborn, but for a mere pot of stew he relinquished his birthright to Jacob. Later Jacob dressed up like Esau and tricked their father, Isaac, into pronouncing the blessing of the firstborn over him. Esau was frantic when he discovered Jacob's masquerade.

Read Genesis 27:41–43. Jacob and Esau went their separate ways after the conflict that defined their relationship. Twenty years passed without any contact between the brothers. During that time, life humbled Jacob, and God changed his name to Israel—allowing him to leave his identity as the deceiver behind. Just as Lisa wanted to reconnect with her friend, so Jacob longed to reunite with his brother.

Read Genesis 32:3–11. What changes do you note in Jacob's attitude toward Esau? ____

____

____

____

Let's see what happened when Jacob and Esau were reunited. Read Genesis 33:1–11.

Jacob humbly approached Esau, knowing he had wronged his brother. Esau, abandoning all pride, ran toward his brother. Stirred with emotion, they both wept. Jacob had been humbled, and Esau had chosen to forgive him. The brothers embraced and let the bad blood that had soured their relationship wash away into the desert sand.

Do you have a relationship that has been severed? If so, which of the brothers can you relate to most as you consider what reconciliation would require?

____

____

____

Whether you need to ask for forgiveness or do the forgiving, do your best to be at peace with everyone (Romans 12:18). As Lisa discovered, a reunion may depend on you.

Chapter Twenty-nine

Divine Refuge

God is our refuge and strength,
an ever-present help in trouble.

Psalm 46:1

It was a warm, sunny day, but a cloud hovered over our hearts and tears rained from our eyes as my husband and I said good-bye to our first child. I'd had a miscarriage. After a wrenching morning and afternoon at the hospital, we returned home to dinner. The evening—a seemingly endless evening—stretched before us.

A trip to the video store or a game of Monopoly might have been appropriate for any other night, but routine pastimes sounded superficial and cold on this day. There seemed to be no right way to spend the remaining hours of the night together.

"Please make this day end," I prayed through my sobs as my husband, Terry, and I hugged after dinner. I nestled into his shoulder and peered out our kitchen window, the backyard in full view.

Ours is a typical suburban backyard, generally well groomed, but that day the most unkempt in the neighborhood. Shaggy tufts of grass covered the wide sprawl of our lawn. They were especially thick under the shade of our favorite birch tree. Looking out the window, I noticed movement—slow, cautious movement. Brown, curious eyes were searching the landscape for a suitable bed. Short, snowy antlers showed the tenderness of their age. Two young deer with the courage to venture outside the bounds of swamp and forest nestled into the cool, comfortable carpet of our yard, the shade of the birch tree providing the perfect place for an evening rest.

As I watched them get settled, I recognized that their resting place was also mine. I praised God as I tiptoed outside to get a better look at my new friends. I spent the next couple of hours snapping photos while Terry videotaped. I cried tears of gratitude as I praised God for allowing me to find rest from my grief in the shelter of my suburban backyard.

I had dreaded an evening destined to be filled only with more heartache. But God answered my prayer for this day to end as He ushered in a new day, no longer characterized solely by sadness but also by the amazing visit from two unlikely friends. God's presence seemed to envelop me in my place among the deer. It was a divine refuge from my heartrending pain.

In the weeks that followed, when I found myself reflecting on the magnitude of our loss, I rested in the knowledge that the one who now cradled the spirit of our baby was the same loving God who cradled me—not just among the deer in our overgrown backyard but also every day.

—Barbara Farland

Embracing God's Truth

After a devastating loss, God provided Barbara a place of rest and relief from an evening filled with sadness when two young deer sought a place of refuge in her suburban backyard.

How is God described in Psalm 46:1? ______________________

____

____

____

Unfortunately, the only way to truly know God as your refuge and strength—to be able to testify that He is an "ever-present help in trouble"—is to journey down the road of suffering, fear, or loss.

Refuge means "shelter or protection, as from danger or distress. . . . A safe place. . . . Something that brings relief, lessens difficulties, etc." King David knew God as his refuge. He sang a song of praise to the Lord after God delivered him from all his enemies. Read some of the words to the song in Psalm 18:1–2. In your Bible, underline each instance where David uses the word "I" or "my," and read the passage out loud.

What words did David use to describe God? ________________

____

____

____

Read the following passages and write the words each person used to describe God when they found refuge in Him:

Moses after God parted the Red Sea and drowned the Egyptians (Exodus 15:1) ____

____

____

____

Hannah after she prayed in anguish for a child and God granted her request (1 Samuel 2:1–2) ______________________________

____

____

____

Samuel after God helped the people of Israel to be victorious over their enemies (1 Samuel 7:12) ______________________________

____

____

____

Reflect on experiences you've had when God was your refuge. Think about a time when He protected you from being laid off from your job, eased your fears in uncertain circumstances, or comforted you through a difficult loss. If you were writing a psalm about your experiences with the Lord, what are some of the words you would use to describe Him? ______________________

____

____

____

In the midst of Barbara's suffering a miscarriage, she and her husband recognized that God had provided relief from an evening of more heartache, grief, and despair when those two precious young deer sought rest under the birch tree. Amid the overgrown foliage of their backyard, Barbara experienced God's divine comfort and rest. She came to know God as her refuge.

Chapter Thirty

Fruitful Overflow

Each tree is recognized by its own fruit. People do not pick figs from thornbushes, or grapes from briers. Good people bring good things out of the good stored up in their heart, and evil people bring evil things out of the evil stored up in their heart. For out of the overflow of the heart the mouth speaks.

Luke 6:44–45 TNIV

We lived in a small town, where I had been working as a CPA in a professional environment for twenty years. When my husband accepted a job in a large city, we decided it would be a good time for me to stay home so that I could be more available for him and our teenage daughter. Secretly, I hoped to be available to God for ministry as well. I was excited as I considered all the ways I might be useful to Him.

I signed up for a women's Bible study, hoping I might find my place of service with the wonderful, dedicated women leading the group. But they wisely required women to be members of the church and to consistently attend Bible study for a year before they could be considered for leadership roles.

Not easily discouraged, I tried to minister to a neighbor who had lupus. I eagerly baked cinnamon rolls and purposefully made my way to her house, certain that she needed me to talk to her about God. But after several attempts, she either really wasn't home or was suspicious of a strange woman on her doorstep, holding a tin pan. I was desperate to serve God. I had been a Christian since I was a young child, and I just knew God really needed me.

I talked to some of the dear women at my church. They lovingly listened to me, welcomed me at Bible study, and prayed with me. One day I came upon Jesus' words in Luke 6:45 (TNIV) and began to ponder them. "Out of the overflow of the heart, the mouth speaks." I thought I was available to serve God, but it seemed God was showing me that I was trying to do it with my own stored-up abilities. I hadn't allowed my heart to be filled up with enough of Him to meet my own needs, much less overflow into service to others.

My perspective immediately changed. I began attending Bible study for the sole purpose of soaking up God's words. I actively listened for His voice as I read my Bible. He began speaking to me through His Word—correcting my misconceptions, revealing blessings, and giving me the opportunity to recognize the good treasures to be found in Him. I sensed that He was asking me to give up the pieces of myself that I held onto for security and artificial confidence. After a lifetime of knowing that I was His daughter, I finally allowed my heavenly Father to love and fill me.

I did eventually find a place of ministry at my church, but only after I had allowed God to fill me up until there was more than enough of His real treasure (rather than my tin pans of rolls) to overflow to others.

Last year we moved again. But this time I didn't start from scratch or with misplaced confidence. I have learned that God will work in whatever areas I offer to Him. I suspect I will make more mistakes along the way, but He is the giver of all good things, and in overflowing quantities.

—Colleen Lohrenz

Embracing God's Truth

Colleen desperately wanted to serve God, but her focus had been on finding a place where she could bless others with her gifts and talents instead of seeking God and allowing Him to work through her. When she began seeking the Lord rather than a place of service, she discovered that true ministry overflows from God's goodness and His work in her heart.

Are you more focused on finding a place to use your gifts and talents or on seeking to know God more intimately? ________________________________

____

____

Jesus made it clear that to bear good fruit in our service to Him, our relationship with Him must be our primary focus. Read John 15:1–4. How did Jesus describe Himself (verse 1)?________________________________

____

____

____

What does God (the Gardener) do to make branches more fruitful?

____

____

____

Pruning is the process Colleen described when she said God asked her to give up the pieces of herself that she had held onto for security and confidence. Is there anything other than God that you cling to for security or confidence? If so, what?

____

Pruning is the painful but necessary process of allowing God to cut away things such as pride and selfishness—traits that keep us from connecting more deeply with Him. Jesus said we must remain in Him if we want to bear fruit. In other words, He is the Vine, and we must remain tightly attached to Him if we want to reach others through our service. So it's important that we be willing to allow God to prune anything that interferes with our connection to Him.

Read John 15:5 and contrast the results of our efforts when we remain connected to Christ and when we are disconnected. ________________

____

____

Read John 15:8–12. Are you taking time to remain in God and store up His Word and love in your heart so that you can allow His love to overflow to others through you? On the scale below, plot your level of connection with God at this time.

•------------------------------------•------------------------------------•

Remaining Attempting Out of Touch

Read John 15:16. When we (the branches), remain tightly attached to Christ (the True Vine), we can minister from His overflowing goodness and love, which are stored within us. Our joy is made complete when we are able to bear much spiritual fruit—fruit that truly lasts and brings glory to God.

Chapter Thirty-one

Peaceful Revelation

You will keep in perfect peace him whose mind is steadfast, because he trusts in you.

Isaiah 26:3

I was employed as a principal in the tax department of a regional public accounting firm that I considered second to none. I worked with wonderful people and earned a great salary. But I was miserable. My two-hour commute and heavy workload left me with little time for my family, myself, or my God. I began spending my long commute time praying for guidance. I cried out to God, asking Him to provide a job that didn't involve a long commute and crushing workload.

I had accepted Jesus as my Savior five years earlier, but I hadn't yet learned to give my worries and troubles to Him. I'd heard people say, "I turned it over to God," but I didn't know how to do that. One day a work situation arose that I was unsure how to handle. As I lay in bed that night, unable to sleep and worrying about what to do, I began to pray: "God, I don't know how to handle this situation, but I know that You do. I'm willing to trust that You will work things out somehow." As soon as I uttered that prayer, I immediately fell asleep.

All I had to do was trust God to work it out? What a revelation! The next day, I began to pray the same prayer every morning. I asked God to show me where He would have me work. Not long after I started to pray daily for guidance, a friend who had been a corporate trainer sensed my dissatisfaction with my work situation and offered to be my business coach—at no charge.

I had no idea whether I needed to find another job, purchase an established accounting firm, or partner with another accountant. I hadn't even considered starting my own firm. My specialty is federal and state tax work, and I didn't feel qualified to handle other services clients would need. Yet through the meetings with my business coach and my prayer times with God, I came to realize that I knew of other firms to which I could refer clients who needed services beyond my expertise—another revelation.

God slowly began to lead me away from a job that had provided great stability in my life to a situation with far less stability—or even a steady paycheck. Wrestling with fear, I nonetheless set a date to go out on my own. I remember sitting in my beautiful office with my resignation letter in hand, wondering if I was making the right decision. But I had prayed for months, and I clung to my faith that God was leading me.

I started my firm with a small group of clients, working in a spare room in my house. During those months of praying, God had placed a number of people in my life who provided business referrals. Each year the business grew by about 50 percent, almost exclusively through referrals.

After five years in business, I purchased a permanent office just three miles from home. In addition to a thriving practice, I have many godly friends, loyal employees, and clients who are a joy to serve. I am able to take time off to spend with my son (when it isn't tax season), and God has provided a sufficient income for me to support myself and my son without having to endure a long commute. I've learned to trust God with my fears and my troubles, knowing that He is faithful and worthy of my trust. That's a revelation that brings me peace, even in uncertain circumstances.

—Darlene Plumly

Embracing God's Truth

Darlene learned to cast her cares upon the Lord, and the peace she gained enabled her to step out in faith and trust God as she made major changes in her life.

In order to truly cast your cares upon the Lord, we have to believe that God has knowledge of and authority over all our circumstances. In other words, we have to believe in the sovereignty of God. Read the following passages and note what you learn about God's ultimate control over all circumstances:

Isaiah 55:8–9 ____

____

____

Daniel 2:20–21 ____

____

____

Romans 8:28 ____

____

____

Ephesians 1:11 ____

____

God is working in all events to accomplish His divine plan. No situation catches Him by surprise; no ruler on Earth is beyond His control. We can trust Him, even when we don't understand the trials we are facing, because His Word promises that He is working everything together for our ultimate good.

One revelation that helps us to maintain peace regardless of our circumstances is that, as believers in Jesus Christ, we can look forward to eternal life in heaven, where the struggles and hardships of this life will be over. Read the following passages and note what you learn about heaven:

John 14:1–3____

____

____

Revelation 21:1–5 ____

____

____

What burden or anxieties are you carrying right now? _______________

____

____

Which of the passages you looked up brings you the most comfort or encouragement at this time? _______________________________

____

____

Turn your burdens over to God. You may not know how to handle life's struggles, but He does. He is sovereign. "Cast all your anxiety on him because he cares for you" (1 Peter 5:7). You can trust Him with all your concerns. That is, indeed, a peaceful revelation.

Chapter Thirty-two

A Message Delivered

We are therefore Christ's ambassadors,
as though God were making
his appeal through us.

2 Corinthians 5:20

I sat on the bare cement floor across from inmates as I helped facilitate a Bible study about spiritual freedom. A group of women from my church had just finished the study, and we felt compelled to share it with women in prison. It is a classroom setting I will forever cherish—a huddle of spiritually hungry female prisoners looking through bars at women who were marveling at the scene unfolding before them.

Five years later, I was still involved in prison ministry. The jail had relocated to a new building, one which had enough space for us to offer Bible studies in meeting rooms. As the gatherings grew larger, we eventually expanded the program to include lectures and music. Countless inmates have attended the Bible study sessions over the years, and I often found myself wondering how many of them continued to seek spiritual freedom once they had been freed from physical captivity.

One spring I decided to attend an evening women's Bible study with a group of friends from my former neighborhood. Our lives had taken us on different paths, but it was a special treat to get back together and study God's Word. After the first week's session, we went to a nearby breakfast joint to catch up and reconnect.

Lighthearted laughter erupted from our table when the waitress, Linda, informed us that the grill and fryer were broken: everything we had ordered had been taken off the menu. Thankful for the opportunity to enjoy one another's company, we graciously ordered sandwiches and salads.

After we were well into our meal, Linda returned to the table and asked, "Have you ladies come from some sort of awesome women's convention?"

"No, why do you ask?" I replied.

"I thought I heard you talking about the good things God is doing in your lives."

"We just came from Bible study," I said with a smile.

With tears in her eyes, Linda told us that she had been drug-free for six months and said that God was changing her heart and life. We invited her to sit down at our table, and we took turns praying for her. Afterward, she proceeded to tell us that just six months earlier, she had been on the street smoking crack. An officer with three criminals in his backseat stopped her, discovered she had a crack pipe, and drove all of them to jail.

"The Harris County Jail?" I asked.

"Yes."

"Did you ever attend a Bible study session with the two Vickys?" (My ministry partner's name is also Vicky.)

"Yes!" Linda said as her eyes brightened. After a brief pause, she exclaimed, "You are the one who wouldn't let me speak!"

As I looked at her more closely, I distinctly remembered a session when a cute little red-haired woman asked to share something with the group. I initially told her no but then sensed the Holy Spirit's prompting to let her share what turned out to be a story filled with tragedy and grief.

I asked Linda if she would share with our group the testimony she had shared that day in jail. She nodded and smiled sheepishly as she began to tell her story. When Linda was still a young girl, her mother died. Linda became hooked on crack the first time she ever tried it and suffered what she believed to be horrific demonic attacks while under its influence. She had lost children because of her drug abuse and neglect: one of her daughters had drowned in a bathtub. Linda had also survived cancer.

As she was speaking, I turned to look at my friends. Everyone had tears streaming down their faces. I flashed back to that day in prison when she first relayed her sad story, and I thanked God that I had followed the Holy Spirit's prompting and allowed her to share. My thoughts returned to the present as she went on to share how God had set her free from her addiction during her incarceration.

The precious red-haired waitress serves as living proof of the freedom God can bring to incarcerated women through His Word. I was overcome with emotion as I recognized that God had not only brought me together with old friends that night but also had brought me to that particular restaurant so I could see a woman who was truly finding freedom as a result of a ministry that began on the cold, musty cement floor of a prison cell.

—Vicky Landry

Embracing God's Truth

Vicky helped start a prison ministry in a county jail. Five years later, God allowed her to meet a woman whose life had changed as a result of that ministry.

Vicky and the other women who ministered to inmates at the jail were able to look beyond the attitudes and choices that had caused the inmates to lose their earthly freedom. They reached out with the message of spiritual freedom through a relationship with Jesus Christ. What preconceived ideas or fears do you have that might make it difficult for you to reach out to women in prison? ______________________________

____

____

Read 2 Corinthians 5:16–19. We are reconciled to God through faith in Jesus Christ. We need to ask God to help us avoid the temptation to look at people merely from a human viewpoint. Regardless of the situation, every person is in need of God's transforming power. We all have fallen short and made mistakes. We all need the freedom and mercy offered through our Savior.

Ask God to enable you to look beyond circumstances or outward appearances and to see the spiritual needs of the people you encounter.

Read 2 Corinthians 5:20. You are an ambassador for Christ. Take a moment to list some people in your sphere of influence who haven't yet accepted the message of reconciliation with God through faith in Jesus.

____

____

Take a moment to consider how you might approach each person on your list with the message of reconciliation. Write down any ideas that come to mind.

____

____

Pray for the people on your list, and ask God for opportunities to act upon your ambassadorship. Some day you just might find yourself celebrating with someone whose life has changed because of what you did.

Chapter Thirty-three

For His Name's Sake

Let him who boasts boast in the Lord.

2 Corinthians 10:17

I felt giddy and excited as I heard the announcement at church that Sunday morning. Our congregation was organizing a trip to Israel and, although I had no idea how we could afford such a trip, I told my husband that I wanted to go.

We were a single-income family with two young children and bills to pay. My husband laughed as he assured me that I wouldn't be going anytime soon.

Smiling, I said, "Well, if you don't mind, I'm going to pray about it."

"That's fine," he replied, "but the answered prayer does not involve a new balance on our credit card."

I felt boxed in. Even if a miracle check arrived in our mailbox, the money would surely be spent on more appropriate things. Yet I continued my prayer: *Please, Lord, I sure would love to be on that plane!*

A few weeks later, while doing my Bible study, I came across some passages in Ezekiel, chapter 36. Verse 37 said, "This is what the Sovereign LORD says: Once again I will yield to the plea of the house of Israel and do this for them." I immediately sensed that this was a personal word from the Lord to me. I continued reading in verse 38: "Then they will know that I am the LORD." God seemed to be telling me that He would answer my prayer and I would be going to Israel—for His name's sake. I penciled "January 14, 1999" along with the word "Israel" next to the passage in my Bible.

Although most of my fellow church members were aware that I didn't have the money to pay for the trip, whenever the subject came up, I couldn't hide my excitement. When people asked if I was going, I responded, "I hope to!" In my heart, I still believed God had spoken to me through His Word.

But as the weeks and months flew by, it was no more likely that I would be going to the Middle East. The itinerary was set, and all those who would be traveling received their tickets. My name was not on the roster. Still, I continued to believe that the words I had read in my Bible were for me. As ridiculous as it seemed, I couldn't shake the sense that I was supposed to be on that plane.

Then it happened. Three days before the scheduled trip, I received a call from my pastor. He said, "Lucille, someone has paid for your trip. You're going to Israel!" Even he was incredulous. He said that someone had bought my ticket, and he wasn't allowed to reveal the person's identity. I hung up the phone and sobbed. To this day I don't know who paid for that ticket.

It was an amazing trip! I was incredibly grateful. I basked in God's goodness at each site we visited. But God wasn't finished confirming His purpose. Three days into our stay, we awoke early in the morning and made our way to the Mount of Beatitudes. It overlooks the Sea of

Galilee. The air was foggy, dew dripped from the flowers and trees, and birds chirped merrily. As we sat on the steps of the beautiful Catholic church that had since been built on that location, I could picture Jesus walking with and talking to His followers.

Our Israeli guide began reading from Ezekiel 36. When he got to verse 38, he said that God answers our prayers for His name's sake, not for ours. My mouth dropped open and my eyes welled up with tears as God once again confirmed the words I'd read months earlier. My presence on the steps of that church reminded every member of my congregation that He is able to answer the prayers of His people. He answered my plea and provided the means for me to go on the trip, all for His name's sake.

—Lucille Zimmerman

Embracing God's Truth

Lucille wanted to join members of her congregation on a trip to the Holy Land. One day God confirmed through His Word that He would answer her prayer and would do so for His name's sake. Those same scriptures were read by the tour guide as Lucille sat on the steps of an old Catholic church in Israel. Once again, God confirmed that He had answered Lucille's prayer in order to bring glory to His name.

God works in the lives of His people so that others will recognize that He is God. A famous work of God is His miraculous parting of the Red Sea when the Israelites were being pursued by the Egyptians. Read Exodus 14:21–28 and write a brief summary of the event. ____________________

____

____

According to Psalm 106:7–8, what was God's purpose in parting the Red Sea? ____

____

Read Joshua 2:8–11. What caused the people of Jericho to fear the God of Israel?

What conclusion had Rahab come to about God (verse 11)?

People might be able to argue about theology or specific interpretations of Scripture, but no one can dispute a personal testimony of God's work in your life. When God answers one of your prayers in a tangible way, as He did for Lucille, take every opportunity to tell others what He did for you. If God provides financially, don't be too proud to tell others of His provision. When He comforts you during a time of loss or empowers you to overcome an addiction, share your experiences whenever you get the chance.

Take a few minutes and write a short testimony of God's activity in your life.

Make known God's almighty power by sharing this testimony with others. Do a little boasting in the Lord (2 Corinthians 10:17), for our God answers prayer and moves on behalf of His people for His name's sake.

Chapter Thirty-four

From the Valley to the Field

Nothing is impossible with God.

Luke 1:37

It was Matt's senior year in high school. I couldn't come to grips with the fact that he wouldn't be playing baseball with the group of kids he'd played with since he was nine. The team had won a state championship when they were ten. They were together for one final season now—all except for Matt. Our son was in Utah, far away from our home in Pennsylvania.

He'd been drawn away from his former passion by the seductive charms of marijuana. As the drug lured him into a deep valley of darkness and deception, Matt morphed from a witty, smart athlete into a hostile and defiant stranger. Fierce standoffs became routine events in our home—between mother and son, father and son, and husband and wife.

The summer before his junior year, he'd been arrested for having drug paraphernalia in his car. More arguments followed. "It's your fault I got arrested," he shouted. "If you hadn't let them search my car, there wouldn't have been a problem! One of the pipes [of three] wasn't even mine."

He started his junior year of high school by having to report regularly to a probation officer. By April, after repeatedly violating his probation, the courts ordered him out of our home. The summer before his senior year, he attended a therapeutic wilderness program in the rugged mountains of Utah. All he had were the clothes on his back and a magazine to read on the airplane. As I watched him make his way through security and disappear down the airport corridor, I wondered when I would see him again.

Matt completed his wilderness program by the end of the summer, but rather than coming home, he was sent to a program in New Mexico. I was tired, tired of the two years of lies and hurt following the discovery of his drug use. But I missed him terribly. I missed the life we'd had together and the young boy he'd been. I was encouraged by the progress he'd made in Utah, and I longed to see the old Matt play baseball one last time with the rest of his championship team.

That fall Matt's classmates settled into their senior-year routine—Friday-night football games, college tours, and the anticipation of prom and graduation. I struggled to know what was best for Matt, but I always arrived at the same conclusion. I desperately wanted my son back.

I cried out to God, and during prayer time in a church service, I appealed to Him again. Though the desires of my heart were loud and clear, my words were barely audible. They tumbled out in staccato syncopation as tears slid down my cheeks. All I could say was, "I just want to see him play baseball." Those simple words were the pleas of a mother's heart for her son's restoration with the knowledge that sports would be a place where he could once again thrive with a sense of belonging amid leadership and teamwork.

God answered my desperate prayer. Matt came home that fall and finished his senior year with his classmates. My son seemed to come back to life as he played baseball with his childhood buddies, advancing to the state championship semifinals and amassing a 25–3 record. The team was a family, a group of guys who played hard, laughed hard, and uplifted one another in victory or defeat. Matt was back. His greatest victory that season was making his way from the valley of darkness back to the field of our dreams.

—*Kathy Pride*

Embracing God's Truth

The allure of drugs pulled Kathy's son away from her and seemed to steal the life from the witty, charming, young baseball player. But God restored her son, and Kathy soon saw Matt return not only to the ball field but also to the game of life.

Read Ezekiel 37:1–3. Ezekiel was led by the Spirit into a valley of dry bones. He was led back and forth among them, perhaps looking for any sign of life. He saw none. What question did God ask Ezekiel (verse 3)?

____

____

We can find ourselves in what feels like a valley of dry bones when a marriage, once flourishing and fragrant with romance, becomes distant and stale; when a church that at one time was thriving and filled with enthusiasm turns stagnant and feels void of God's presence; when a child, once alive with potential and joy, becomes ensnared by the dark world of drug addiction. In those times, we may be the ones asking, "Can these bones live?" Have you ever felt like you were in a valley of dry bones? If so, explain. ________________________

____

____

Read Ezekiel 37:4–10. What did God tell Ezekiel to do (verses 4 and 9)?

____

____

____

When Ezekiel spoke words of restoration and faith over the dry bones, a rattling sound could be heard, and there was movement among the scattered skeletal remains. He then spoke, as God commanded, to the wind. One can imagine that Ezekiel's knees rattled, too, as the breath of life brought the restored army to its feet.

Read Ezekiel 37:11–14. Israel's rebellion against God left the people feeling like dry bones—parched, thirsty for God's presence, and longing for their homeland. This vision was given to Ezekiel so that the hope of God's people would be restored.

What in your life seems hopeless? Take a moment to present that situation to God. Write a prayer in the space below. ____________________

____

____

____

Kathy was, in effect, standing in the middle of the valley of dry bones as she begged God to restore her son's life. Our God can bring even the driest bones to life. He can restore a marriage, bring revival to a church, and carry a young man from the darkest valley back to a place of restoration and victory—on and off the ball field.

Chapter Thirty-five

A Moving Confirmation

Lead me in the right path, O Lord. . . .
Make your way plain for me to follow.

Psalm 5:8 NLT

I'd been struggling through a difficult period in my life, and my parents urged me to move back in with them while I took some time to heal and regroup. But I'd been living on my own in Nashville for eight years, and moving back in with my parents in Texas would be humbling, at best. Not to mention, the move meant quitting my well-paying job and leaving behind the many friends I'd made in Nashville. Yet for some time I'd felt that the true calling in my life was to lead worship through music, and I couldn't shake the sense that this move would give me opportunities to do that.

While discussing my options with my mom, she said, "Why don't you throw out a fleece?" Not sure of what she meant, I looked up the story of Gideon in the book of Judges, chapter 6. Gideon placed a fleece on the ground outside his home and asked God to confirm His instructions by using the fleece. God responded and confirmed that He would do as promised and save Israel by Gideon's hand—which He did. *But God doesn't work like that anymore,* I thought. Yet even as I entertained the thought, something deep inside was telling me not to place limits on God.

Skeptical, I prayed: "If You want me to move to Texas and pursue worship-leading, then let this house sell for the asking price by Thanksgiving" (which was only about six weeks away). The next day I listed my house privately, without a "For Sale" sign in the yard, never believing it would sell in six weeks during a real-estate slump in the area.

Well, God acknowledged my "fleece." Two weeks after listing the house, I received three offers in one day—all for more than the asking price. The closing date was set for two days after Thanksgiving. At that point I knew that if I didn't move, I'd be disobeying God. Just two months after asking the Lord for answers, I was loading up a trailer and, at age twenty-seven, moving back in with my parents.

Three weeks later, however, I still hadn't found a job and began to contemplate moving back to Nashville. I called a friend and explained all that had happened. He pessimistically asked, "If you believe God's talking to you so much, why don't you just ask Him to give you a job leading worship by the end of the week?"

"Well, I would," I responded jokingly, "but it's already Tuesday night, and that isn't allowing God much time to work." But after hanging up, I kept thinking about his suggestion. Partially from curiosity but mainly out of desperation, I asked God to give me a position leading worship by the end of the week.

The next day, as I was scouring the Internet for jobs, I received a call from the pastor of a church about twenty minutes away from my parents' house. He'd seen one of my postings online and said his church was looking for a part-time worship leader. I almost fell out of my chair! Looking up to the sky, I said, "Are You kidding me?!"

I accepted the position and now lead worship part-time. I still have questions about God's long-term plans for me, but I know He has clearly spoken, and that knowledge allows me to rest in a time of change.

—Debbie Forrest

Embracing God's Truth

Debbie was struggling to know for sure, as she considered moving from Tennessee to Texas, that it was God willing her to go. God confirmed His will by responding to Debbie's "fleece" when He made it possible for her to sell her home, and He confirmed that she was where He wanted her to be by providing a job.

Read the story of Gideon and his fleece in Judges 6:33–38. Israel's enemies joined forces and crossed the Jordan River, preparing to fight. Led by the Spirit, Gideon blew trumpets and sent messengers to call the Israelites to battle. But as everyone prepared to fight, it seems Gideon became fearful.

Look at Judges 6:15 and note what you learn about Gideon.__________

____

____

____

What promise did the Lord make to Gideon in Judges 6:16? ____________

____

____

____

Gideon knew he couldn't lead Israel to victory on his own. As the army prepared for battle, he asked God to confirm that He would indeed save Israel. He placed his wool fleece on the ground and waited. Perhaps, like Debbie, he doubted whether God would respond to his request.

According to verse 38, how much dew did Gideon wring out of the fleece? ____________________

____

____

____

Now read Judges 6:39–40. Why do you think Gideon was concerned that God would be angry with him for requesting a second confirmation?

____

____

____

Gideon was pushing it and he knew it. God had already promised to be with him in battle. He'd revealed the future result of the battle. But Gideon was wrestling with doubt and fear. He needed to know for sure that God would empower him in battle, so he asked God for yet another sign and God responded mercifully. He again confirmed that He would be with Gideon and the Israelite army.

Have you ever laid out a "fleece" by asking God to confirm a direction for you? If so, what were the circumstances and what happened? ____________

____

____

____

We have to be careful about testing God and asking for confirmation, for without faith it is impossible to please God (Hebrews 11:6). But when we are paralyzed by fear and can't discern God's voice, He will often confirm His will if we are truly seeking to follow Him. Then get ready to move!

Chapter Thirty-six

A Heart's Longing

Delight yourself in the LORD and
he will give you the desires of your heart.
Commit your way to the LORD;
trust in him and he will do this.

Psalm 37:4–5

Shortly after the birth of our first son, I felt a deep longing in my heart to adopt a little girl from China. As the years passed, my husband and I had three more sons, and the desire to adopt faded. But one day, when I was scrapbooking with a group of women in our community, a young woman passed around a photograph of a little Chinese girl who had recently been adopted. As I looked intently at the photo, I felt that familiar stirring in my heart. I was convinced that my husband and I were supposed to adopt a girl from China.

In the months that followed, God placed a number of couples in our path who either had adopted or were in the process of adopting. I attended a Christian concert with our oldest son and was moved to tears when the lead singer announced that he and his wife had recently adopted a child from China. Through songs, comments from friends, and His Word, God seemed to confirm His desire for us to adopt.

As I was listening to a Christian radio program one day, the speaker read Matthew 13:45–46, which says, "The kingdom of heaven is like a merchant looking for fine pearls. When he found one of great value, he went away and sold everything he had and bought it." I sensed God telling me that our little girl would be a pearl of great value and that although it would cost us dearly to bring her home, she would be worth it. Later that day I discovered that the name Meghan, which my husband, Chris, had always wanted to name our daughter (should we have one), means pearl.

I shared the information with Chris, but he quickly reminded me that our finances were extremely tight. In addition, China's government had minimum income requirements for families who were interested in adopting. We didn't meet them. I didn't know how to overcome the obstacles before us, but I believed and kept praying that the Lord would somehow provide a way for us to adopt our pearl.

The following Mother's Day, Chris gave me a beautiful pearl ring as a reminder that we were trusting God to provide the funds needed for us to adopt. We didn't know how the Lord would supply the money, but we began the qualification process in faith, believing that God would go before us. After making the commitment to move forward, however, unforeseen circumstances made our finances even tighter. Although I was discouraged by the setback, Chris and I prayed and waited in anticipation for God to work.

That November some friends tragically lost their baby just before she was born. I was deeply touched when they presented us with a check for one thousand dollars in honor of their daughter. The next week another couple gave us a check for four hundred dollars. Two weeks later we received a grant from Shohanna's Hope, an organization that provides grants for families whose finances might prevent them from adopting a child. I had applied for the grant earlier that year.

God worked in amazing ways to provide for us. But despite all the exciting monetary gifts, we still hadn't accumulated enough money to pay all the expenses. With the agency deadline just a few days away, I prayed that God would somehow supply us with an interest-free loan so that we could complete the adoption without the burden of too much interest. I held tightly to my faith that the Lord had placed this child on our hearts and that He would somehow provide us with the means to pay for her adoption.

The following Sunday, at church, I told one of my friends about our struggle to pay the agency fees. Imagine my surprise when her husband walked up to me a little while later and offered to loan us ten thousand dollars without interest. God had answered my prayer! Needless to say, I was overwhelmed. God enabled us to pay all the fees and expenses, interest free. To top it off, when Chris calculated our total income at the end of the year, we discovered that we had met the Chinese income requirements for adoption. Words are inadequate to express my gratitude, both to God and to all the generous servants who responded to His prompting.

With the economic needs met, our focus shifted to the logistics of traveling to China to get our daughter. My husband's work commitments conflicted with the usual time frame for picking up a child after a referral. But our social worker fasted and prayed with me, petitioning God to somehow enable us to pick up our daughter in five weeks rather than the customary six- to eight-week period. Amazingly, we were able to schedule our trip five weeks from the referral date. According to the social worker, that hadn't happened before and hasn't happened since.

We now have a beautiful, bright little girl running around our home. Our boys adore her and have never once shown signs of jealousy. Her name, of course, is Meghan.

—Barbara Goulet

Embracing God's Truth

Barbara and her husband faced many obstacles as they sought to adopt their daughter, Meghan. But they believed God was in control and held tightly to their faith that He would somehow enable them to adopt their pearl of great value.

What does Mark 11:22–24 tell us about the power of faith and the role of prayer when we are faced with mountainous obstacles? ________________

____

____

____

Read Hebrews 11:1. How did Barbara's actions during her wait reveal her faith? ____

____

____

____

If someone were to read about your response to the challenges you're facing right now, what evidence would they find of your faith? ________________

____

____

____

Take time to pray right now that God will strengthen your faith. Read Proverbs 3:5–6. If you don't already have this passage memorized, write it on an index card and memorize it this week. Ask God to help you trust Him more fully with your future.

Chapter Thirty-seven

Illuminating Darkness

He has sent me to proclaim freedom for the prisoners and recovery of sight for the blind, to release the oppressed.

Luke 4:18

By the time I'd backed into the mailbox at the end of our driveway for the third time, my driving had become the joke of the neighborhood. My excuses were a cover for the simple truth—I didn't see it!

I'd lived a storybook life. My husband's swift climb up the corporate ladder had allowed me to fulfill my dream of being a stay-at-home mom, spending my days caring for our three sons. But my perfect world began to crumble as I faced what seemed like an ugly monster from a childhood nightmare.

At the age of thirteen, I'd been informed by an ophthalmologist that my retinas were deteriorating. He'd warned me that no one could predict how long I would have my sight. At thirty years of age, I began to see that prognosis turn into reality.

First, I struggled with night blindness. Next, my peripheral vision began to diminish. Within a few short months, my vision was no more than one could see while peering through a keyhole. Finally . . . I was engulfed in complete darkness.

I sank into a pool of self-pity. After all, my sons were two, four, and six years old at the time. They needed their mommy. "This isn't fair!" I cried to God as I shook my fist. I pounded my pillow and begged Him to help me face my dark world. His silence seemed to intensify my anguish. Feeling lost and confused, I collapsed in my dark prison, surrounded by bars of fear and bitterness.

When a friend called and told me that her church was having a service that would be followed by a time of prayer for healing, I quickly accepted her invitation. This is my answer, I thought. This is where I'll receive a miracle!

But I was miserable and angry when I arrived at church. Distracted by my personal pain, I couldn't focus on the service. I resented the people in the congregation. I wanted to scream at the top of my lungs, "You have no problems compared with what I'm facing! Do you know what it's like to realize you'll never see the smile on your child's face again?" Tears streamed down my cheeks. My heart was as cold and hard as the metal folding chair on which I sat.

Then I heard these words, a mixture of power and tenderness: "Seek first the kingdom of God and His righteousness, and all these things shall be added to you" (Matthew 6:33 NKJV). A quick sigh escaped from my lips, and my tears stopped flowing. The words entered my heart like a floodlight and revealed the ugly source of my pain. I'd been consumed with my desire to see again. I'd become an expert at seeking a cure. But in that moment, God urged me to seek Him. Like a child finding her mother after being lost in a crowded store, I flung myself, my life, into the arms of God. My heart answered an emphatic yes to His invitation. His love warmed me like a soft blanket, and soothed away the cold desperation.

In the months that followed, God scooped up the broken pieces of my heart, dusted them off, and gently and lovingly placed each piece in its proper place. His Word became my cane on which to lean. His wisdom guided my steps and gave me the confidence and courage I needed to move forward.

When sighted, I was blinded to His love. It was only through my blindness that I gained the vision to walk in true freedom.

—Janet Perez Eckles

Embracing God's Truth

As Janet tried to adjust to her dark world, she recognized that she was unable to find her way alone. Her blindness illuminated her need for God's comforting presence to guide her. When she accepted His invitation, He lovingly led her to a place of peace, where she found freedom from the fear and bitterness that had consumed her heart.

Have you ever faced a situation that caused you to feel imprisoned by fear and bitterness? If so, describe the circumstances. ____________________

____

____

____

____

Read Luke 4:14–21. Jesus made it clear that He was sent to fulfill the words of the prophet Isaiah. According to verse 18, what specific work was Jesus anointed to do during His time on earth?____________________

____

____

____

____

Before Jan encountered God at her friend's church, she was imprisoned by fear and bitterness. She went to the service that day seeking to regain her eyesight. But she discovered a love that opened the eyes of her heart instead.

Let's look at the verses Jesus quoted that day in the synagogue. Read Isaiah 61:1–3.

Whether your heart is broken, you're grieving a loss, you're held captive by fear, or you are overwhelmed by a spirit of despair, God can meet your need. What do you need from Him right now? ______________________________

____

____

____

____

Your loving heavenly Father is beckoning you to seek Him. If you'll accept His invitation, you'll gain spiritual vision, a sense of peace, and a new freedom that lifts you above your circumstances.

Chapter Thirty-eight

A Good Education

Train a child in the way he should go,
and when he is old he will not turn from it.

Proverbs 22:6

My daughter had gone to public school since kindergarten. She'd gotten good grades, had great teachers, and made many friends. So my husband and I were shocked when she approached us with the idea of being homeschooled during the summer before her fifth-grade year.

We initially dismissed the idea, but a few days later she presented us with a list of reasons why she felt homeschooling would be best for her. Determined to get our attention, she asked us to pray about the idea before we made a decision. Although we were skeptical, we agreed. I don't remember many of the reasons listed on that paper, but as my husband and I prayed, a deep sense of peace came over both of us.

Feeling terribly inadequate and a bit fearful, my husband and I decided to talk with other homeschooling parents to find out what resources were available and how much of a commitment was required. As we gathered information and continued to pray, we became convinced that God was calling us to homeschool our daughter. She was ecstatic when we shared our decision. She jumped up and down and then sang praises to God as she danced around the house. I wish I could say I shared her enthusiasm.

After beginning our new academic journey a few weeks later, my husband and I attended a homeschooling seminar. We met ordinary parents just like us. Many high-school-aged homeschool students were also at the conference. They were clean-cut, well-mannered, and extremely talented. They spoke publicly with confidence. As we sat in the audience listening to their presentations, my husband and I had the same thought: We need to talk to our son about homeschooling. He had just entered high school.

That evening we shared what we had seen at the seminar with our son and asked him to pray about the possibility of finishing high school at home. Within a few days he said that he, too, felt God calling him to be homeschooled.

I was excited and afraid at the same time. Fifth grade seemed possible, but I didn't feel equipped to teach high school curriculum. I knew I would have to seek assistance for some subjects, but I was willing to try. I contacted our local Home School Association and discovered that they had a list of resources to assist parents.

God's provision was amazing. Several people living right in our community were willing to work with our son. He even had the privilege of visiting a scientist's office to complete his science labs. An English teacher worked with both of our children to help them polish their writing skills. We took numerous field trips, and our son and daughter both participated in a number of local theatrical productions. God provided everything we needed for their education.

Our daughter wants to become a journalist and has a wonderful command of the English language. Our son recently completed his master's degree and is serving in the army as a combat medic. Both have strong educational and spiritual foundations.

Our homeschooling journey was not always easy. There were times when the kids rebelled against my authority. I often worried that they wouldn't be adequately prepared for college. But through the years, God answered our prayers as we sought His will and followed His lead.

—*Wendy Savino*

Embracing God's Truth

As Wendy sought God's guidance regarding the education of her children, He led her and provided everything she needed to meet their individual needs.

Read Judges 13:6–8. When Manoah and his wife learned they would have a son, what was Manoah's prayer (verse 8)? ______________________________

____

____

____

____

____

____

Manoah understood that his child had unique needs, and he asked God to teach him how to raise his son. Do the children in your life have unique needs? What are they? ____

____

____

____

Proverbs 22:6 tells us to "train a child in the way he should go." Take a moment to pray as Manoah did. Ask God to teach you how to train, influence, and meet the unique needs of the children in your life.

Chapter Thirty-nine

Beneficial Battle

We know that in all things God works for the good of those who love him, who have been called according to his purpose.

Romans 8:28

I sat on an examining table looking at my entire family as they gathered in a tiny office at M. D. Anderson Cancer Center. The doctor's words, "quality of life," made my mind reel. How could this be? This happens to other people, not me. I don't have time for cancer!

My husband, Doug, and I ran our own business. We were up by four o'clock every morning, and we both worked hard just so we could be back home by midafternoon each day. I couldn't imagine how Doug could possibly manage the work by himself. I just wanted to find out what needed to be done and get on with my life.

"I will survive this," I insisted, interrupting the doctor. God had been faithful to me my entire life. I knew He would see me through cancer. I always thought I had strong faith, but I didn't realize how much my faith would be tested in the coming months. The diagnosis of stage-three breast cancer ushered in a long year of tests and exhausting treatments. Yet God provided for me in ways I could never have anticipated.

Meals mysteriously appeared in coolers by my back door. I received notes of encouragement from people I hadn't heard from in years. Our church women's group prepared meals and took turns stopping by to visit and help with household chores. My daughter rearranged her schedule and took me to almost all my treatments. My daughter-in-law prayed with me before my treatments. One day, when I was feeling poorly after a round of chemo, my son took off work to sit at my bedside. I remember feeling a mixture of pride and sadness. I kept thinking, *A mother does this for her son, not the other way around.* My family sacrificed and supported me through the entire ordeal.

Doug ran our business by himself that entire year. Sometimes our son or son-in-law would help. During Thanksgiving, a particularly busy time for us, some of our grandchildren even pitched in. My heart ached to see Doug working so hard. I wanted to help him. I knew he was exhausted, but he never once complained. It was clear that God saw him through that year.

Through the entire ordeal, God was faithful to work all things together for good, just as He promises us He'll do. Despite the doctor's initial grim prognosis, I responded so well to treatments that I came through the ordeal needing only a lumpectomy. After five years, I'm still cancer-free, and the doctor calls me her miracle patient. I call the entire experience a blessing.

I now am able to thank God for my cancer. He worked a lot of good through my battle. Family relationships were strengthened. My healing served as an example of the power of prayer and faith. I developed a special bond with my church community, and I had countless opportunities to encourage, minister, and offer hope to others. But most of all, God's loving care was made more real to me than ever before through the outpouring of support and care that I received from my family and friends.

—*Mary Ferguson*

Embracing God's Truth

Mary's friends and family rallied to support her as she battled her illness. She did not want to have cancer, but as she reflects on her ordeal now, she is able to thank God for all He did during one of the most difficult trials of her life.

Read James 1:2–4. Many of us spend our lives trying to avoid pain or hardship. Yet what benefits do these verses indicate we will gain by enduring trials? ____

____

____

____

____

____

How have you seen God work good through difficult situations you've faced?

____

____

____

____

____

What does Philippians 4:4–7 tell us to do in every situation? What are some specific ways you can do these things in your life? ________________

____

____

____

____

____

The next time you face an unexpected trial or a hardship, ask God to help you learn to rejoice in the fact that He is near and at work in your circumstances. Do your best not to be anxious. Instead, present your needs to God. Ask Him for peace and for eyes to see the good that He will bring out of even the most tragic circumstances.

Chapter Forty

Sweet Generosity

They gave as much as they could afford and even more, simply because they wanted to.

2 Corinthians 8:3 CEV

After being out of town for almost a week, our family finally pulled into the driveway at nearly three in the morning. Abandoning the hitched trailer and van in the front drive, we wearily made our way to the house.

Our son Jared and our daughter-in-law, Johanna, had spent a few days at our house while we were gone because of some heating problems at their apartment. The house was completely dark, and I fumbled my way through the darkness to our master bathroom. I immediately noticed that something was different. "Hey, honey," I called to my exhausted husband, Steve. "Come look at our bathroom!"

As he entered the room, he said, "There's a new shower curtain . . . and someone scrubbed the curtain rods too."

"And the sinks and faucets are sparkling," I added. "Those little buggers," I exclaimed, referring to Jared and Johanna. "They cleaned everything for us!" Turning around toward the bedroom, I stopped and asked Steve, "Does anything look different to you?"

"What do you mean?"

"Our bed," I replied. "It's higher!" Looking closer, I said, "And you know, I think the mattress is different!"

"It can't be," my husband said as he peeked under the corner of the sheets. "Oh, my, it is!" he exclaimed with widening eyes.

"How did they . . . Where did they . . . With what did they . . . " I stammered and finally concluded with, "Those little buggers!"

I can't honestly say that I was enthusiastic. On the contrary, I was initially ridden with guilt. My thought was, *We should be doing this for them!* The parable of the widow's mite came to mind, as did the one of the rich man taking the poor man's sheep.

"They can't afford this!" I exclaimed to my husband. "They need that money for themselves!"

How undeserving I felt. But they hadn't stopped at just the mattress; they bought us a new mattress cover, flannel sheets, pillows, and even a new padded toilet seat.

My husband responded wisely, "But it gives them joy to do this for us. We'd gotten used to our lumpy old mattress. I'd forgotten how uncomfortable it was when I offered to let them sleep in here. Don't take away their joy of giving. Try to find joy in receiving."

I slept soundly that night on our comfortable new mattress. When I awoke, I realized that midweek services would be held at our church that evening, so I would get to see my son and daughter-in-law. Throughout the day God worked on my heart, helping me to overcome the pride that kept me from graciously accepting their gift.

That evening when I saw them, my eyes filled with tears as I said, "I don't know whether to hug you or holler at you! I am so overwhelmed!"

At that, they excitedly shared their reasons for the gifts and their experience in pulling off such a venture. They were genuinely thrilled to have surprised us.

"It was Johanna's idea," Jared confessed. "She said that you both give so much to your children that you deprive yourselves."

Johanna smiled sweetly and added, "I figured you've probably needed a mattress for years. After Jared and I slept on it, we realized that you'd just gotten used to it being lumpy and lopsided."

Their sacrifice meant even more when I discovered that it was initiated by my daughter-by-marriage. The deeper blessing was the evidence that she really had accepted our family as her own. I embraced them both with tears and thanked them profusely. It was a gift far beyond any expectations.

—Maribeth Spangenberg

Embracing God's Truth

Maribeth was overwhelmed when her son and daughter-in-law used their meager resources to surprise her with a badly needed new mattress. But they didn't stop there. The blessing was made even sweeter when they cleaned the bathroom and purchased several luxury items as well. The young couple's sacrifice expressed their love for Maribeth and Steve, and the love of Christ was also apparent in their sacrificial, unexpected gifts.

The young couple gave generously to Maribeth and her husband, more than they could really afford to give. But it brought Jared and Johanna great joy to surprise his parents with new bedding and a sparkling clean bathroom.

In 2 Corinthians 8:1-4, the apostle Paul wrote about the generosity of the Macedonian churches. Read this passage and note the circumstances those churches were experiencing when they chose to support Paul's ministry.

____

____

____

Paul wrote about these churches (which included the Philippians) again in Philippians 4:15–18. What more do you learn about the generosity of those churches from this passage? ____

Read the following passages and note what you learn about the importance of being generous in your giving.

2 Corinthians 8:7 ____

____

2 Corinthians 9:7 ____

____

Read 2 Corinthians 9:10–11 and note what you learn about the purpose of God's financial blessings in the life of a believer. ____________________

____

God's Word makes it clear that His children are to be generous. Is there someone you can bless with an unexpected gift? If so, take a moment to jot down some ideas about how you might surprise that person like Jared and Johanna surprised his parents. ________________________________

____

Ask God to help you grow in the grace of giving. As you become a person who gives what you can on all occasions—sometimes even beyond what others would consider practical—people around you will lift thanksgiving to God. You'll have the joy of knowing that you are wearing the sweet fragrance of generosity. It is an aroma that is pleasing not only to others but also to God.

Chapter Forty-one

Comforting Refuge

He who dwells in the shelter of the Most High will rest in the shadow of the Almighty. I will say of the LORD, "He is my refuge and my fortress, my God, in whom I trust."

Psalm 91:1–2

As my husband and I walked along the dirty sidewalks of graffiti-ravaged Mexico City, I was overwhelmed by my surroundings. The walkways were broken and crumbling. Tall security walls—with jagged, broken glass bottles cemented in along the top—surrounded every home. Stray, filthy dogs wandered freely along the dusty, littered streets. I couldn't imagine our daughters, who were staying with grandparents back home in Missouri, playing around the trees where these animals were marking their territory.

Only a month earlier, missionary work was the farthest thing from our minds. My husband was a real-estate agent, and I was the children's coordinator for our church. I had never been outside the

United States in my life. In fact, my only traveling experiences were holiday visits to relatives' homes two states away. Yet here we were, considering a move to live and work at Niños de Mexico, which is a children's home near Mexico City.

Our church had recently hosted a speaker from the home. The organization offers a loving, stable home environment—including food, clothing, and an education—for children who would otherwise live on the streets or die of starvation. As my husband and I listened to the presentation, we both felt a strong desire to get involved. After a series of meetings, much prayer, and consultation with our pastor, we traveled to Mexico City to tour the home before deciding whether to accept a position with Niños de Mexico.

I continued to absorb the sights and sounds of Mexico as the director of the home explained the different areas of ministry that were available to us. I was quiet, but when my husband and I were back in our room that evening, I shared my concerns. I was struggling to understand what God could possibly have in store for our family in Mexico. I just couldn't get used to the idea of our girls being exposed to the wild dogs. But my husband, who had been to a Third World country on a previous mission trip, reassured me that we would get used to the dogs and that God would protect our daughters. We prayed together, asking for God's guidance before we went to bed. Still, as I drifted off to sleep that night, I felt confused and full of doubt about our move to Mexico.

The next morning my husband and I sat down together to do our daily devotion. The Scripture passage we read that morning was Psalm 59:14–16: "They return at evening, snarling like dogs, and prowl about the city. They wander about for food and howl if not satisfied. But I will sing of your strength, in the morning I will sing of your love; for you are my fortress, my refuge in times of trouble."

As soon as I read those verses, I sensed God reminding me that He is my refuge. I knew He was reassuring me that no matter what dogs might prowl around us, we would always find strength in Him. For the remainder of our visit to Mexico, I felt an indescribable peace that allowed me to trust God and relinquish my will to His.

When we arrived back in the United States, God guided us through the sale of our home, the purchase of a vehicle that could handle the poor street conditions near the home, and the difficult task of telling our friends and family that we were moving to Mexico to serve God by caring for children.

We joyfully served at Niños de Mexico for three years. Obedience wasn't always easy, but because I was willing to step out in faith and allow God to lead me down the path He had chosen for me, I discovered the comfort and strength that come from dwelling in the shelter of the Most High God.

—Lisa O'Hanahan

Embracing God's Truth

Lisa can testify that God is a fortress and refuge for His people. When we face times of uncertainty or trouble, we can cry out to God for help. He is faithful to comfort us and walk with us through even the darkest seasons of our lives.

What circumstances cause you to feel vulnerable or afraid? ____________

____

____

____

____

____

David was the second of Israel's kings. During his reign, he faced many enemies and fought many battles. Toward the end of his life, David wrote a song celebrating God's faithfulness to shelter him and deliver him from all his enemies. Read a portion of David's song in 2 Samuel 22:1–4, and note all the descriptions of God that David included in these passages.

____

____

____

____

____

Like Lisa, King David had experienced the shelter of the Most High God (Psalm 91:2). The next time you feel vulnerable or fearful, call out to your Rock, your Fortress, and your Deliverer. And when the trial is over, you, too, will be able to thank the Lord for His faithfulness as David did.

Chapter Forty-two

Sacrificed Desire

Delight yourself in the LORD *and*
he will give you the desires of your heart.

Psalm 37:4

When an afternoon business appointment was canceled, I found myself with a free afternoon in an Orlando, Florida, resort. Most people would be elated to have unexpected free time in one of America's beloved vacation spots, but I felt gloomy and depressed.

It was the anniversary of my heartbreaking miscarriage. My husband and I had married in our late thirties and, in our forties, joyfully found ourselves expecting a baby. When we lost our baby, I feared that I had lost my one chance at becoming a mother.

In an effort to avoid the pain, I focused on a speech I was preparing for a women's Bible-study group. The topic was sacrificial giving. As I wandered through the beautifully landscaped walkways of the resort, I felt God whisper to my heart, "What about you? Are you willing to sacrifice?"

Sacrifice what? I asked silently.

Then, as clearly as if He were standing next to me, God said, "Your dream of having a child."

I was overcome with shock, sadness, and despair. Sacrifice my dream of having a child? I choked back tears. How could He ask such a thing?

Flustered, I ran to my car. Trying to hide from God's heartbreaking request, I escaped to Downtown Disney—an outdoor haven for shopping and entertainment. But as I walked along the shop-lined sidewalks, mothers with young children were everywhere. I gulped as a young father twirled his darling little girl, proudly dressed up in a princess costume. Children's faces filled with joy and wonder were around every corner of that magical place. I wanted to collapse in the middle of the street and sob.

Still running from God, I returned to my hotel room and ordered a personal-size pizza. Planning to submerge myself in a movie and eat away my pain, I reached for the remote control. But before my finger could press the power button, I sensed God urging me to spend time with Him.

I didn't feel like doing anything with God, especially praying or reading my Bible. Yet . . . relenting, I let go of the remote. For the next several hours, I sat on the bed clinging to the two-hundred-thread-count sheets, crying and wrestling with God.

I sensed that He was continuing to press me with the question, "Are you willing?"

Am I willing to sacrifice having a family to do whatever You want me to do with my life? I can't believe You'd ask that of me. Who am I if I am not a mother? My husband would be a great father. My parents would love to have another grandchild . . .

I protested and argued. My heart ached as I struggled to lay my hopes and dreams at His feet. I pleaded, *Why do I have to sacrifice this dream?*

"Are you willing?" He persisted.

Finally, around midnight, exhausted and terribly disappointed, I surrendered.

About a month later, I began having some health issues. After a number of visits to the doctor, I was informed that I was pregnant. Me? Pregnant?! How could that be? Repeated tests confirmed the results. That December, my husband and I humbly and tearfully welcomed our beautiful boy, Luke, into the world. We named him after the reference of a passage we quoted throughout the pregnancy: Luke 1:37, "Nothing is impossible with God."

—Karen Granger

Embracing God's Truth

Karen felt God asking her to sacrifice her dream of having a child. Even though she wrestled with Him and resisted, she eventually surrendered to God's will. Having given up her lifelong dream of being a mother, Karen never dreamed that God planned to give her the child she longed for before the end of the year. Perhaps Karen needed to relinquish her dream of having a child before she was ready to become a mother surrendered to God's will and plan.

Karen's story reminds me of the time when God asked Abraham to sacrifice his son. God had promised to bless Abraham with many descendents through his son Isaac. Yet when God asked Abraham to sacrifice the boy, Abraham trusted God enough to obey.

Read Genesis 22:1–5, 9–12. According to verse 12, what did Abraham's willingness to sacrifice the son he loved reveal? ______________________

____

____

____

____

Do you have a dream or passion that you would find difficult to surrender to God? If so, explain. ____

____

____

____

____

God didn't actually require Abraham to sacrifice his son. But in the process of laying Isaac on the altar, Abraham revealed his trust and reverence for God. The greatest desire of his heart was to obey God.

What additional information do you learn about Abraham's trust in God from Hebrews 11:17–19? ________________________________

____

____

____

____

Sometimes, as with Abraham (and Karen), God will not actually require you to sacrifice your dream. Other times, as Abraham reasoned, God might resurrect a sacrificed dream at some later time. Some dreams or desires are never realized. But if God asks you to sacrifice something, you can rest assured that He has a reason for that request.

If we delight ourselves in the Lord more than any dream or passion, the Lord Himself will become the greatest desire of our hearts. And that's a desire He'll never ask us to sacrifice.

Chapter Forty-three

Avowing Trust

When I am afraid,
I will trust in you.

Psalm 56:3

Answering my phone, I heard my husband's frantic voice urging me, "Come quickly! Something is very wrong!" Only fifteen minutes earlier, he had left my office to get Chinese take-out for dinner. "My right hand won't grasp the steering wheel! My right leg won't move. I think I'll fall if I try to get out of the car!"

I grabbed my cell phone, car keys, and purse. Hanging up, I turned to a coworker. "What's that acronym for stroke?"

She responded quickly, "F.A.S.T.—Face, Arms, Speech, Time. Ruthanne, it's 9:16 p.m. Don't forget!"

Running out a side door, I dialed my husband's cell phone number. Amazingly, I remained calm. "Bob, when you hold out both arms, are they even?"

"No," he said, his voice revealing his alarm. "My right arm is drooping!"

"Can you see your face in the mirror? Look at your smile. Is it crooked?"

"It's too dark!" His next words began to slur.

"Bob, listen to me! Hang up! Call 911 right now!"

As I drove, I prayed: "God, I trust You. I trust You!"

At the restaurant I whipped into a parking space and ran to one of the EMTs already on the scene. I identified myself, and we sprinted the short distance to my husband's red hatchback. The paramedic poked his head in through a window and asked, "What seems to be wrong?"

Bob's words were thick and indistinct. The paramedic looked at me. "Does he normally talk this way?"

"No," I answered emphatically, adding, "Symptoms began at 9:16 p.m."

Strong hands lifted Bob from the car, onto a gurney, and into the ambulance.

Realizing that he couldn't even give the EMT his name, I grabbed his planner off the car seat. The ambulance was already moving, so I ran behind and threw the planner containing his ID through the doors as they were closing.

"Mom!" Our twenty-one-year-old son was running toward me. "What's going on? Dad called."

I handed him his dad's car keys and said, "Get Dad's car to the house, and then meet me at Florida Hospital South!"

"Mom, should I call people to pray?"

"Yes!" I responded quickly and got into my car.

Near the hospital, one of our church pastors phoned me. "What can I do for you?"

Perfect timing, I thought as I scanned the grounds with its multiple parking garages. "Tell me where to park!"

Careful, clear directions followed; then the pastor prayed for Bob and for me. Getting out of my car, I had a clear sense that I must declare my trust in God. Feeling a little uncomfortable with the pastor still on the phone, I announced, "God, I trust You. Regardless of the outcome, I trust You!"

I followed the signs to the emergency room. Once there I scanned the crowded facility. Two nurses, an aide, and a doctor surrounded Bob's bed. They'd discovered a clot in the left side of his brain. The doctor informed me that Bob was a good candidate for a clot-bursting medication that can stop the effects of the stroke and possibly reverse some symptoms. In the same breath she told me that it could also cause his brain to bleed and kill him.

I looked at my husband. Our eyes connected. No words were needed. I granted permission. Lord, You know! You care! I trust You! I release him to You!

The IV medication was finished at 12:10 a.m., just six minutes before the three-hour treatment window closed. All we could do now was wait.

With my husband in ICU, I returned home. I crawled into bed, and as I drifted off to sleep, I again declared my trust in God.

The next morning, as I walked into his hospital room, Bob greeted me in his normal voice. He lifted his right hand, waved, and elevated his right leg. No residual effects from the stroke.

I whispered a prayer, "God, I am so grateful!"

—Ruthanne Dorlon

Embracing God's Truth

As Ruthanne's husband was having a stroke, she was able to declare her trust in God even though she was frightened and unsure of what the future would hold for her husband and her family.

Ruthanne's declaration of trust in God is reminiscent of three Jewish men who boldly avowed their loyalty and trust in God as they faced what seemed a certain and untimely death at the hands of King Nebuchadnezzar.

The king had created an enormous gold statue and issued a proclamation that everyone in the province was to bow down and worship it. But three

Jewish men named Shadrach, Meshach, and Abednego chose to disobey the king's command. Read Daniel 3:13–18.

According to verse 17, what did the three men expect and hope that God would do for them? ____

____

____

Shadrach, Meshach, and Abednego knew God was able to save them. And even though they hoped He would rescue them, they also seemed to understand that, for whatever reason, He might not choose to do so. What does their statement in verse 18 reveal about their loyalty and trust in God?__________

____

____

Read Daniel 3:19–23. God is able to do anything, and He did rescue the men from the fire. He also protected Bob from any lasting effects from his stroke. But there are times when God does not rescue us from the fires and challenges we face.

As Bob was being rushed to the hospital, Ruthanne proclaimed her trust in God regardless of the outcome. Have you ever declared or are you able in a current situation to declare trust in God even when you're confronted with the possibility that He will not bring about the result you hope for or expect? Give an example. ____

____

____

Nothing is impossible for God (Luke 1:37). There is no question that He can work in whatever situation we face. The next time you face uncertain circumstances, remember Ruthanne and the men standing before the fiery furnace. True faith is revealed when we are able to avow trust in God, regardless of the outcome.

Chapter Forty-four

The Door of Hope

I will make the Valley of Trouble a door of hope.

Hosea 2:15 NCV

Have you ever noticed that God often does some of His most amazing work through the gravest of circumstances? A few years ago our family spent Thanksgiving on a mission trip in a small border town of Mexico. Our visit included leading a Bible study and doing landscape work at a home for unwed pregnant girls. The name of the home is Puerta de Esperanza, which means Door of Hope. The meagerly furnished stucco house is a refuge for many young girls who had been lured into prostitution or a sexual relationship because of the hopelessness of their poverty and living conditions. Some were victims of sexual assault. Pregnant and rejected by their families, the girls (between the ages of twelve and sixteen) had been left to fend for themselves.

Many of the girls we met had wandered away from their faith in God. Their mistakes or victimization brought public shame and rejection. But in Hosea 2:14–15 (NCV), God spoke of His rebellious and broken people of Israel, saying, "I will lead her into the desert and speak tenderly to her. There I will give her back her vineyards, and I will make the Valley of Trouble a door of hope." Regardless of the circumstances that brought the girls to the home, God can take what appears to be inescapable trouble and transform it into a gateway to a better life.

Each girl at the home is offered the opportunity to complete her education—a rare privilege for girls like these in Mexico. She is taught how to care for her child and is given a safe place to live, food to eat, and job training. Inside the Door of Hope, the girls find safety, support, and a fresh start.

—*Mindy Ferguson*

Embracing God's Truth

Perhaps you've never been pregnant and alone. Maybe you've never felt the sting of your family's rejection. But can you recall a time when you made a mistake that shrouded you in shame or chose a path that limited your options? If so, explain. ______________________

____

____

____

____

____

____

____

Regardless of how far away we stray, our heavenly Father offers us hope and restoration. For example, read Luke 15:11–24.

The youngest son rejected his father and squandered his inheritance on wild parties and self-indulgence. What caused the young man to return to his father (verses 14–17)? ____________________________________

____

____

____

____

____

When the money was exhausted, the humiliated, hungry young man returned home, hoping he would be accepted as a hired servant. How was the rebellious son greeted by his father (verse 20)?____________________________________

____

____

____

____

____

As soon as the young man's silhouette appeared on the horizon, his father ran to him, threw his arms around him, and kissed him. The wayward child was welcomed back, not as a servant, but as a son.

What assurance do we have according to Hebrews 4:14–16? ____________

____

____

____

Seasons of rebellion often land us in the Valley of Trouble. But God can use even our greatest mistakes to woo us to a place where He tenderly convicts us, gently cleanses us, and mercifully restores us. We will find mercy and grace in our time of need. Our God can transform even the deepest Valley of Trouble into a door of hope.

Chapter Forty-five

Heavenly Minded

Set your minds on things above,
not on earthly things.

Colossians 3:2

"Beth! Beth! Help!" Startled out of an exhausted sleep, I heard my father's voice frantically calling me. Certain he'd fallen out of bed, I jumped up in a panic and ran to the dining room that had been temporarily turned into his bedroom.

"What's the matter? Are you okay?" I asked, surprised to see him in bed.

"I can't find my glasses."

What?! I thought. *You're yelling in the middle of the night because you can't find your glasses?* I searched for a couple of minutes and then told him, "It's two a.m.—we can find them in the morning."

"No, I need them now! I can't see what time it is!" Dad responded with a note of distress in his voice.

I knew from his tone that he was not going to go back to sleep until the glasses were found, so I began crawling around on the floor. *Lord Jesus, please help me honor my father and walk in a way worthy of my calling,* I prayed silently as I dove under the rented hospital bed. Thirty minutes later, I finally found his glasses—wrapped up in his tangled bedsheets.

A month after my dad moved in with us, our two-year-old granddaughter also came to live with us permanently. At fifty-one, I found myself caring for my sick, elderly father and a high-energy toddler. *Hey, wait a minute, Lord! I'm a singer. I gave up a secular music career so I could sing for You full-time. Now You want me to babysit?* I felt confused and disoriented in my unexpected role.

Dad was hospitalized often with a variety of ailments. Because of his confused mental state, I had to stay with him around the clock. My granddaughter and I spent many days and nights in the hospital, where I learned to be grateful for children's programs and portable DVD players.

Even at home I rarely slept through the night. "Beth! Beth!" Dad would call at all hours with one emergency or another. I repeatedly begged God to help me finish the race well, to give me patience, and to empower me to always treat my dad with respect—even when I was exhausted and frustrated.

My husband supported me throughout that long year by often fending for himself and taking care of my father's financial affairs. Everything in my life seemed to be on hold: my marriage, my music, and even my time with God. My mother's piano sat in a corner, gathering dust. I longed to sit down and play, but I only knew how to play the guitar, not the piano.

One morning I decided to try to spend a few minutes reading my Bible. Remembering a friend's suggestion that I put scriptures to music, I sat at the piano and found myself writing a song on an instrument that I didn't know how to play. As I sang the chorus to my new song from Colossians 3:1–3, "Set Your Mind on Things Above," I knew it was a gift from my heavenly Father to help sustain me.

The Lord inspired me to write a number of scripture songs that year. Whenever I had a free moment, I'd run to the piano, close my eyes, and be transported to the feet of Jesus as I sang one of my new songs for Him and to Him. Without fail I felt refreshed, renewed, and at peace.

My beloved father died in late October. I miss him, but I am grateful that God relieved his suffering. It was the hardest year of my life but also the most fulfilling. Sometimes I think I hear Dad calling, "Beth! Beth!" But now it reminds me to set my mind on things above, for I know my dad's eyes are beholding Jesus—without the aid of glasses!

—Beth Williams

Embracing God's Truth

As circumstances stretched Beth beyond her normal limits, her heart's desire was to spend time in the presence of God. Even when her schedule was dominated by the needs of people around her, she spent the few moments she had worshipping and seeking to be close to Him. She discovered the benefits of learning to set her mind on things above.

Read Colossians 3:1–4. Why do you think it's important to have both your heart and your mind focused on Christ? ______________________________

____

____

____

____

Sometimes our hearts and minds are out of sync. Our hearts long to be in the presence of our Lord, but our minds are occupied with the obligations and desires of our earthly nature. Write down the earthly things listed in Colossians 3:5–8 that can distract us.

Look at the list you wrote for the previous question and underline the items that tend to bid for your affection or attention.

As Beth prayed and worshiped God in the midst of difficult circumstances (set her heart and mind on things above), she found the refreshment and strength she needed to be a loving caretaker for her father and granddaughter.

Read Colossians 3:12–14 and note the virtues God will help us to display when we set our hearts and minds on Christ.

As we seek God with our hearts and direct our thoughts toward His purposes, we are empowered, as Beth was, to compassionately respond to people around us with gentle patience and loving-kindness—even when their demands seem trivial or their expectations unreasonable.

Ask God to help you set your heart and your mind on Him and to fill you with the virtues you listed above.

Chapter Forty-six

Giving Extravagantly

Who am I, and who are my people, that we should be able to give as generously as this? Everything comes from you, and we have given you only what comes from your hand.

1 Chronicles 29:14

In May 2005 our church embarked on a capital campaign for a much-needed children's building. My husband and I were aware of many financial testimonies, and we wanted to be witnesses to the world of God's provision. We wanted to "tell the next generation the praiseworthy deeds of the Lord, his power, and the wonders he has done" (Psalm 78:4). We stepped out in faith, pledging beyond what was logical or, perhaps, even sensible.

We began by surrendering our dream of taking a cruise for our tenth anniversary. Our finances were tight, but we committed to give to the building campaign, above our regular tithe, while continuing our commitments to missionaries and other organizations. We were excited about sacrificing for God. But finances got even tighter when, seven months after our commitment, our third son was born. A short time after that, my husband's employer decided to stop paying for employee health insurance. Instead, the company increased salaries. That meant we had to tithe on the higher salary while also increasing our expenditures for health insurance. It didn't seem fair. But we remained faithful to our commitment.

We settled into a simple, strictly budgeted lifestyle and began saving for Christmas in October 2006. One afternoon some termites flew out of a post in our backyard. Treating the infestation ate up all of our Christmas savings. I struggled to understand why God would allow creatures to eat our home when we were sacrificing and giving extravagantly.

By June of the following year, we were beginning to get back on our financial feet when a random accident with our dog led to an unexpected and very expensive bill. The budget got tighter, and our sacrifices got bigger. Fear and doubt crept in. I thought, *Are we the only ones doing this? What were we thinking?*

When our finances were at their worst, we discovered just before we went to church one Sunday morning that our bank account was overdrawn. We wept as we sang the praise songs during the service. I wondered, *What did we do wrong? Why is God punishing us? We simply want to give Him more. Shouldn't we have enough money?* We were devastated when we had to get money from our equity line of credit, because we had always strived to remain debt-free.

As I wrestled with God over our financial situation, I realized that we hadn't run out of money. We had equity in our home. God reminded me that when the termites we'd discovered a year earlier had returned (four days before our warranty expired), the company paid for a second treatment and completely repaired our wood floors. Those floors had needed to be replaced before we ever discovered termites. In addition, my husband had recently been promoted. As I prayed, it became clear to me that through each struggle, God had provided for our needs—and beyond.

On February 12, 2008, two months before the end of our church's three-year campaign, we were able to write a check to fulfill our pledge. We also paid off our home-equity loan. Our journey was much more difficult than we ever could have imagined, but today we have a testimony of God's faithfulness. We can indeed tell the next generation of the praiseworthy deeds of our God!

—*Shelby Young*

Embracing God's Truth

Shelby and her husband sacrificed and gave extravagantly to the building campaign at their church. They had a deep desire to honor God with their wealth and to teach their children about God's faithfulness. Although they encountered numerous unexpected struggles along the way, God was faithful to supply all their needs throughout their three-year journey of faith.

The decision to give extravagantly to your church or other ministry organizations should be prayerfully approached. Offerings should be given out of gratitude and love for the Lord. King David set a wonderful example for us when he gave an extravagant offering toward what we might call a capital campaign to raise the resources necessary for building the first temple.

Read David's prayer in 1 Chronicles 28:2–3, 6. What desire had been on David's heart, and what was God's response? ______________________________

____

____

Although David was not the one to build a temple for the Lord, he had a deep desire to see it come to pass. He prayed that God would provide everything that was needed, and he was willing to sacrifice by giving lavishly toward the project.

Read 1 Chronicles 29:1–16. What was David's attitude regarding his possessions? ____

____

How does David's mind-set challenge you? ______________________

____

____

Read verse 17 and note the spirit with which David made his offerings.

____

____

Read 2 Corinthians 9:6–7. Do these verses challenge you or comfort you? Explain your answer. ______________________________

____

____

Take a few moments to pray about the level of your current giving to the body of Christ. Consider David's generous offerings and the spirit in which he gave them. Ask God if you need to make any changes in the amount of your offerings or in your attitude toward giving. Maybe you need to be more consistent, regularly giving an amount that you prayerfully determine ahead of time. Or perhaps God is urging you to step out in faith, as Shelby's family did, giving extravagantly for a specific project.

What do you sense God telling you about your giving? ______________

____

____

Read Luke 6:38. Give generously to God with a cheerful heart. Sacrifice out of gratitude and a deep desire to honor God with your wealth. Chances are good that you've been given more than you really need. Any amount you offer to God is simply a portion of what has come from His generous hands. No one can give more extravagantly than our God.

Chapter Forty-seven

Peace in the Thanksgiving

Do not be anxious about anything, but in everything, by prayer and petition, with thanksgiving, present your requests to God. And the peace of God, which transcends all understanding, will guard your hearts and your minds in Christ Jesus.

Philippians 4:6–7

My beautiful, compassionate, soon-to-be-teenage daughter was struggling academically as well as socially at school. We had moved her from a private school with small classes to the public middle school close to home. The transition was a difficult one for her, and as her struggles to fit in extended beyond the first school year, I began to fear that her self-esteem and confidence would be permanently damaged.

I had heard about a Moms in Touch International group that gathered to pray for their children and their schools on a weekly basis. After investigating the organization, I decided to begin praying with a group of mothers from my daughter's school.

One morning, after praying with my prayer partner, I shared my amazement at the significant difference I'd noticed in my daughter's attitude and performance in school since I'd joined the group. I was puzzled by the change, since I had always prayed daily for both my children.

My wise friend responded, "It's in the thanksgiving."

In the thanksgiving, I repeated to myself. As I pondered her words and thought about the changes I'd seen in my daughter, I began to realize something. The Moms in Touch format includes time at each prayer session for members to thank God for His activity in the lives of their children. Because I paused to thank Him for even the most subtle changes or victories, I was able to recognize the work God was doing in my daughter's life and in mine.

I was familiar with Philippians 4:6–7, but as I picked up my Bible to read the passage carefully, it took on deeper meaning for me. "In everything, by prayer and petition, with thanksgiving, present your requests to God. And the peace of God . . . will guard your hearts and your minds in Christ Jesus."

I'm still learning to take the time to praise God for His activity in my family. But I've discovered that praying with thanksgiving changes my focus from what I am waiting for to what He has already done. I've found that cultivating a thankful mind-set creates a peaceful heart within me. Appreciation and gratitude instill hope.

Are you like me, lingering in God's waiting room, desiring His peace? It's in the thanksgiving.

—Glenda May

Embracing God's Truth

Glenda discovered that coming to God with our challenges, with our focus on His activity and blessings, creates a greater sense of peace—regardless of the circumstances.

Let's read about a challenge Paul was facing as he wrote the words that spoke so strongly to Glenda. Read Philippians 4:1–3.

Apparently Paul had become aware of a conflict between two women at the church in Philippi. These dedicated servants had ministered side by side with Paul, yet they were at odds with each other for some reason. The contention was such that they needed assistance in resolving their differences. Paul pled with the women to settle their disagreement.

Have you ever had a conflict with someone that went unresolved for a long period of time? If so, what impact did that conflict have on you or the people around you? ____

____

____

____

Paul went on to describe the antidote for such conflict. Read Philippians 4:4–7.

Glenda discovered a greater sense of peace when she presented her concern for her daughter's well-being to God with an attitude of thankfulness. It appears that Paul was urging Euodia and Syntyche to apply the same approach to restore harmony to their relationship.

As we bring our burdens (or conflict, as in today's scripture reading) before God, Paul urges us to rejoice (for the Lord will return soon), to be gentle, and to prayerfully make our appeal to God with gratitude for all that we've received from Him.

Read Philippians 4:8 and note the things we should focus on to cultivate an attitude of thanksgiving as we pray. ______________________________

____

____

____

We will inevitably encounter circumstances that burden us or make us feel anxious, and at times we will have disagreements with others. But if we want to maintain a sense of peace, not being anxious about anything, it's important that we, "by prayer and petition, with thanksgiving, present [our] requests to God" (verse 6).

Read Philippians 4:9 and note the result of that approach to the challenges we face. ____

____

____

____

The next time you are anxious or struggle with unresolved conflict, put Paul's advice into practice. Like Glenda, you'll discover the peace of God, which transcends all understanding (verse 7). There is peace in the thanksgiving.

Chapter Forty-eight

Blessed Perspective

The LORD gave,
and the LORD has taken away;
blessed be the name of the LORD.

Job 1:21 NKJV

It was the day after Thanksgiving. People were bustling with plans and activities. They were Christmas shopping, putting up decorations, and celebrating with loved ones. Yet there I sat in the quiet, reflecting on the events that had recently unfolded in my life.

In the course of just a few years, my grandfather had been diagnosed with cancer; my father developed heart problems; and my younger sister was diagnosed with a disorder of her central nervous system and, shortly thereafter, gave birth prematurely to a baby with heart problems. As if that weren't enough, my first husband and I adopted a sweet little boy whose birth mother's drug and alcohol habit made the first year of his life quite challenging, my mother was diagnosed with uterine cancer, and I went through a painful divorce. Now I was married to a wonderful, godly man, and we were expecting conjoined twins that probably wouldn't live after they were born.

I was just a few weeks along when we discovered I was pregnant. My new husband, Craig, seemed to know from the beginning that we were having twins. But neither of us could have been prepared for our first visit to the doctor. Yes, we were having twin girls; but after viewing the ultrasound, our doctor also informed us that they were joined at the chest and were sharing a heart. A visit to a specialist confirmed the diagnosis. We were told that if they survived the pregnancy, their lives would be short—days, perhaps only hours.

In the beginning, I was angry. I didn't feel spiritual. I felt as though God had taken away part of my life. How could He give us what we had prayed for and then bring us to the point of utter despair? Just eight weeks into pregnancy, we were told that our babies were going to die!

The pregnancy has progressed, as have our emotions. I am twenty-eight weeks along, and it appears that we will make it to delivery. Each day has become a gift and an answer to many prayers. At first I prayed that God would take the babies early, thinking it would be easier to lose them before we became emotionally attached. But as time passed, Craig and I began to ask God to allow them to be born alive so that we could see and hold them for a short time before their heart gives out.

As of right now, we don't know what will happen, but we know that God is at work. I don't understand. But God does, and He knows exactly what He's doing. Through it all, He has been with us, and He will sustain us. Even better, He is not through with us. I think of Job. He lost it all—everything. But in the end, he was given more than he'd ever lost. Who else can do that but God?

We've named the girls Avonlea Rose and Lily Anna. I don't know how much time I will have with them or what lies ahead, but I can rest in the fact that I know the God who holds the future—for all of us.

—Paige Stewart

Embracing God's Truth

Paige and her family had recently experienced a lot of heartache and illness that was difficult to understand and endure. As she anticipated the birth of her conjoined twins, Paige clung to her faith that God was at work, even when her life seemed to be consumed with suffering and difficulty.

God doesn't promise that His followers will live pain-free, easy lives. Unfortunately, suffering and pain are a part of life here on Earth. Paige found encouragement and strength from reading about the life of Job. Read Job 1:1–3 and note what you learn about him. ______________________________

____

____

____

Read Job 1:13–22. How did Job respond to the tragedy that seemed to invade his life all at once? ____________________________________

____

____

____

Job considered all that he had to be gifts from God—His to give and His to take away. But Job's troubles didn't end with these losses. Read Job 2:1–10.

Consider your response to tragedies and loss in your life. Do you tend to become angry and resentful, like Job's wife, or are you more inclined to take Job's perspective? Give an example. ______________________________

____

____

____

God again brought prosperity to Job, giving him twice as much as he originally had (Job 42:10). But Job's greatest asset was his ability to recognize that neither his abundant possessions nor his calamity were outside the knowledge and supervision of God.

As Paige reflected on the many hardships in her recent past and awaited the birth of her twin girls, knowing her time with them would be (at best) short, she attempted to adopt the same perspective as Job.

Avonlea Rose and Lily Anna were born December 22, 2007. They lived only a few days. But through all the joy and heartache Paige and her husband experienced, everyone around them was inspired as the couple maintained an outlook like Job's: "The LORD gave and the LORD has taken away; blessed be the name of LORD" (Job 1:21 NKJV).

Chapter Forty-nine

Hope-Filled Joy

"I know the plans I have for you," declares the LORD, "plans to prosper you and not to harm you, plans to give you hope and a future."

Jeremiah 29:11

Compared with our family home in Ohio, the small Texas town with dirt streets and prickly cacti dominating the landscape seemed like a set from an old Western film. So helping to construct an apartment building for a deserving group of teachers at a mission in Roma, Texas, was an adventure. As our church-sponsored mission trip came to a close, we never imagined that the rustic town would soon become our home.

In the months following our trip, the old hymn "I'll Go Where You Want Me to Go" kept playing in my mind. I continually found myself singing the words and committing to do whatever and go wherever God directed me. One day, as I reflected on our trip to Roma, I sensed God asking me, "Do you mean those words?" My heart pounded as I quietly replied, "Yes, Lord, I do."

I immediately felt that God wanted our family to serve Him in Roma. Anxious thoughts consumed me, but it was important to me to be obedient. I shared my experience with my husband. We knew there was a need for a children's home in the area, and we began to pray for wisdom and confirmation. After several days of praying with friends, fasting, and praying some more, we both felt strongly that we were supposed to return to Roma to build a children's home.

We sat down with our kids, ages three, nine, and eleven at the time, and told them that we believed God was calling our family to serve Him in Roma. Amazingly, I don't remember a single objection. We began making preparations for the move. The following Sunday our church had a special service focused on surrendering to God's will. During the prayer time, my husband was overcome with emotion as our entire family stood with our hands raised in surrender to God's plan. The Elkins family was unified and set on obeying God.

The following week my husband gave notice at a job he had loved dearly and worked at for fifteen years. We put a "For Sale" sign in the front yard of what had been my dream home. We dealt with many fears, but we knew God would faithfully take care of the details. Our house sold quickly. Before we knew it we had loaded all our belongings into a rental truck and were headed for Roma. As we pulled onto the highway, a beautiful double rainbow appeared directly ahead of us. The peace of God washed over me. I knew we were on the right path and rested in the fact that God knew the plans He had for us in Texas.

We were greeted in Roma with a beautiful sunset and a warm meal freshly prepared by the mission team. We enjoyed a time of prayer and fellowship and then moved our belongings into the one-bedroom trailer that would serve as our home for several months.

The first order of business was purchasing some land. We found a beautiful piece of property on a hillside at the edge of town. The local people warned us that we would never be able to deal with the owner, but we knew God could handle him. Before approaching the property owner, we walked around the entire piece of land, praying and claiming it for the Lord's work. As we did this, my husband felt that God gave him the exact amount of money to offer for the property. We were nervous, but we made the proposal. To everyone's surprise, the man told us to draw up the papers, and he would sign them. We left his office that day exclaiming praises to our Lord.

Once the land was secured, the foundation was poured and our family worked diligently to construct the children's home. I learned to hammer, operate large saws, hang drywall, and even shingle a roof. Our two oldest children helped by handling domestic chores and caring for their little sister. Our family made many sacrifices, but we learned to trust the Lord through many uncertain, trying, and sometimes frightening circumstances.

God was faithful to supply just what we needed at each stage of construction. Whenever funds came in, we drove sixty miles each way for supplies. Somehow we always returned home with our truck loaded for a few more days of work. Throughout the project, workers skilled in cabinetry or construction always seemed to arrive to help just when we needed them. The timely arrival of workers and funds was a great testimony of God's faithfulness, not only to us, but also to our children. We developed tremendous faith in God's sovereignty and power.

When the 3,400-square-foot home with seven bedrooms and three bathrooms was finally complete, we named it the Home of Joy—with Joy standing for "Jesus first, Others second, and Yourself last." The name served as a constant reminder of our priorities.

God sent us many troubled teenagers. Most were failing school. Some had even been in trouble with the police. But we set boundaries, extended lots of unconditional love, and taught them about a God who offers hope.

We had some great success stories. Sadly, we had our hearts broken a few times too. But each experience built our faith. Through the Home of Joy, we exposed teenagers whose situations often seemed hopeless to the God who has a plan for each of their lives—plans to prosper them and not harm them, plans to give them hope and a future. It truly was a home of hope-filled J.O.Y.

—*Annette Elkins*

Embracing God's Truth

The Elkins family impacted many teenagers' lives because Jesus was their top priority. Although you may never be called to sacrifice as their family did, serving God should be a priority for you too. But to truly be effective in ministry, you need to develop an intimate relationship with Jesus.

Read John 15:1–5. What insight do you gain from these passages about the importance of making your relationship with Jesus a priority?

____

____

Read John 15:9–10. In the King James Version, the word *remain* in verse 10 is translated "abide." According to this verse, how do we abide in God's love?

____

____

Read John 15:11 and note why Jesus gave these instructions. ____________

____

____

Read John 15:12–13. What command did Jesus give us that will cause our joy to be complete? ____

____

____

Ultimately our joy wells up and shows on the surface when we serve God by pouring our lives into the people around us. What changes do you need to make to better reflect the J.O.Y. the Elkins family experienced as they adopted the motto Jesus first, Others second, and Yourself last?

Chapter Fifty

Refining Delivery

The righteous cry out,
and the LORD hears them;
he delivers them from all their troubles.

Psalm 34:17

"You're pregnant," the doctor declared, looking at my fifteen-year-old daughter, Katherine, who had been complaining of a stomachache. I was stunned. Katherine began to scream and sob. I wanted to fall down and beat the floor, but I knew I had to remain calm.

During our long drive home, I sensed God telling me to be silent and hold Katherine's hand, which I did. It was all I knew to do. When we arrived home, I called my husband and told him the heartbreaking news. He immediately came home, and we all sat down and cried together.

I was ashamed, embarrassed, and concerned about what people would say. I remember going to bed that night and praying that

Katherine would miscarry. My next thought was abortion—no one would have to know, and we could go on with our lives. The thought made me sick. I ran to the bathroom, looked into the mirror, and sobbed. You see, Katherine was adopted. I asked myself, *What if her birth mother had opted for an abortion?* I knew I couldn't think that way anymore. My heart ached with grief and pain as I went to her room, curled up with her, and spent the night holding my daughter in my arms.

In the coming days, as I sought God for direction, I sensed Him telling me that I needed to take my eyes off myself, stop worrying about what people were going to say, and make Katherine and her baby my priority. Knowing we needed guidance, we joined a support group that included two other mothers and their teenage daughters. The encouragement and counseling we received helped mold Katherine's decision to give her baby up for adoption.

Although Katherine had made some poor choices that led to her pregnancy, I was proud of her decisions regarding the baby. Those decisions and their consequences were difficult. She endured stares, whispers, and pointing throughout her pregnancy. Yet in spite of it all, Katherine remained focused on making sure her baby was healthy.

She worked with an agency that offered open adoptions and selected a wonderful couple we both believed would love the baby and allow Katherine to be involved in the child's life. The adoptive mother and I were with Katherine the day of her delivery. The attending nurse, a kind woman, told us that she had helped deliver babies for girls associated with an adoption agency in Austin, Texas, during the late 1980s. I immediately felt God's presence with us, because the agency the nurse referred to was the same one that had coordinated Katherine's adoption in 1987. We all knew we were making the right decision.

My granddaughter recently turned four years old. We are able to visit her and even stay with her birth family from time to time. God carried my daughter through every difficult step of her pregnancy, and she is being refined by His strong and gentle hands. She's doing great, has a wonderful life, and loves her daughter dearly. I adore my daughter and granddaughter. I know God loves us all, and He can deliver us through any situation our future holds.

—Marilyn Maynard

Embracing God's Truth

Marilyn was devastated when she learned that her fifteen-year-old daughter was pregnant. She and Katherine cried out to God, and He was with them, refining them both through the consequences and pain of their ordeal.

We all have sinned. We all fall short of the glory of God (Romans 3:23). But there's nothing more humbling—and potentially refining—than when we fall publicly. As Katherine's clothes became taut around her midsection, her sin became evident to everyone she encountered. Katherine and Marilyn were broken and crushed in spirit as they turned to God for strength and guidance during the pregnancy.

Malachi 3:3 speaks prophetically about Jesus. How is He described in this verse? ____

____

____

Through Marilyn and Katherine's long ordeal, the Refiner used the consequences and pain of public humiliation to uniquely refine and purify them. Marilyn was stripped of the need to project an image of perfection to others. Katherine's crushed spirit led to greater dependence upon Christ.

Read Psalm 34:17–18 and note how God responds to the cries of His people. ____

____

____

____

When Marilyn and her daughter cried out to God, He was faithful to draw them close and comfort them with His presence. He provided a couple who not only have lovingly cared for Katherine's baby but have even allowed Katherine and Marilyn to be involved in the child's life.

How has the Refiner used painful events, even consequences of poor choices, to purify you? ____

____

____

____

Write out the words of Psalm 3:3 below. ____

____

____

____

The next time you stumble or fall, cry out to the Lord. He will hear you. He will be your shield and deliverer. As Katherine and Marilyn both discovered, God does some of His greatest refining work in the process of delivery.

Chapter Fifty-one

Treasured Days

All the days ordained for me
were written in your book
before one of them came to be.

Psalm 139:16

It was a clear brisk December day. High winds were bearing down on the Gulf of Mexico. Pinecones rolled along the sidewalk, and palm fronds swayed wildly. I hadn't walked the tree-lined street in front of my parents' home on the coast of Florida since my near-fatal accident two years earlier.

That afternoon my twelve-year-old niece, Sara, dropped by with her heart set on making a three-layer cake with frosting from scratch. I had missed her more than I could express during my eighteen-month recuperation in North Carolina, and nothing could have pleased me more than taking a walk along the bay together before we began baking.

We slowly made our way down the street. I steadied myself

with my cane, and our cheeks were rosy from the gusts of cold air. We mouthed words that were barely audible over the rushing sound of the wind and broke into laughter. And suddenly, it was as though my mind took a snapshot of that moment. Our delightful reunion was worth the pain that grew more intense with each step.

With kind concern, Sara asked, "Are you all right, Aunt Barbara?" Before I could respond, she continued, "Maybe I should go back and ask Grandpa to come pick you up."

I wanted to finish our walk, so I assured her that I would be fine after I sat down for a few minutes. I spotted a small platform next to a mailbox, so we sank down onto the cold concrete seat. We huddled together to stay warm and glanced across the bay at the barrier island that spanned the horizon. Seagulls glided over the weathered docks searching for food.

I pulled Sara's lightweight jacket closer to her chin as I admired her flawless complexion. Her eyes danced with excitement as she talked about her plans to decorate our cake with mounds of rich, buttercream frosting.

When she stopped talking, I noticed we were both shivering. I didn't want to send her back to the house for help, so I prayed that my dad would know that I needed him and would come to our rescue. I shared the content of my prayer with Sara, and within minutes we saw the familiar bright-red pickup pull away from the house and make its way up the street toward us. As the truck pulled over near the mailbox, Sara jumped up and ran to the door shouting, "Grandpa!"

"Need a ride?" he quipped, holding back a chuckle.

"Grandpa, how did you know we needed you to come pick us up?"

As we climbed in, he grinned (enjoying his hero status) and said, "Oh, you'd been gone awhile, and I wanted to make sure my girls were all right."

I gave Sara a wink as she settled into the warm cab with her Grandpa.

"You girls want to go for an ice-cream cone?" he asked.

Sara and I yelled, "Yeahhhh!" Sara wrapped her slender arm around her Grandpa's as he held the steering wheel with steady hands. So there we were, all together again—safe, warm, happy. Sara looked back and forth at our faces as we drove along the bay, singing in harmony to the southern gospel music that was playing on the radio at full concert volume.

For a moment I reflected on all the pain and struggle God had brought me through during my eighteen months of rehabilitation. My heart swelled with joy as I treasured the events of the day and recognized my abundant blessing of more time with my family.

—Barbara Parentini

Embracing God's Truth

After being involved in a near-fatal accident, Barbara is grateful for the opportunity to make more memories with her family. She treasures the days she has, recognizing that they can end at any time.

When was the last time you took a long walk with a friend, baked a cake with a child, or took a vacation? ______________________________

____

____

Most of us live hectic, busy lives. It's easy to say "I'll take some time with the kids next week" or "I'll put off that vacation until a better time." But what warning do you find in James 4:13–15? ______________________________

____

____

James 4:14 (NLT) says, "Your life is like the morning fog—it's here a little while, then it's gone." Even a thick fog that demands our attention and frustrates our morning commute quickly evaporates without a trace.

Look up the following passages and note what you learn about the days we have on Earth: ____________________

Job 14:5 ____________________

____

____

Psalm 139:16 ____________________

____

____

The number of your days on Earth is known only by God. The length of our lives is not for us to control. But we can control what we do with the days we've been given. We can take time to stroll along the beach with beloved friends. We can say yes to a child's invitation to a tea party or spend an afternoon baking a cake with an enthusiastic niece or nephew.

Read 1 Peter 4:7–10. What could be a greater use of your days here on Earth than serving and loving people around you? The time will come when your days end, and your life will be summed up in a few words etched in marble. What words would you like to summarize your life? ____________

____

____

Ask God to reveal any changes you need to make for that summary to become a reality. Love deeply, offer hospitality joyfully, and serve others with a heart overflowing with the grace of God. Treasure each day, for He alone knows the number you have remaining.

Chapter Fifty-two

Mercy Road

The faithful love of the LORD never ends!
His mercies never cease.
Great is his faithfulness;
his mercies begin afresh each morning.

Lamentations 3:22–23 NLT

When I moved to Southern California, I noticed that most of the streets along the freeway had Spanish names. One exit always caught my attention because, unlike the others, the street was named Mercy Road. I often wondered where the road went and how it had come to be named Mercy. Sometimes I would consider taking the exit just to explore the road and discover its destination. I never took the time to actually do it, but the name caught my attention whenever I passed it.

On my way to a meeting one night, traffic on the freeway was at a virtual standstill. After traveling about two miles in thirty minutes, I decided it would be best to exit. Sitting in traffic even along my alternate route, I turned on the radio to find out what was causing the delay. Apparently someone had entered the freeway heading in the wrong direction at the Mercy Road exit. The mistake caused a multiple-car accident.

In spite of my agitation with the traffic, I recognized that the situation painted a vivid picture of God's mercy toward His people. When we make poor decisions—even those that impact the lives of many innocent people—he has pity on us and comes to our aid. I had to admit that I'd made my share of poor decisions that caused anxiety or problems for me and others around me. Yet God was always quick to show mercy. He helped me through my messes and took care of the people affected by my mistakes. He held my hand as He cleared away the collisions and helped me find my way back to the right road.

As I considered how many hundreds of people were sitting in traffic, waiting for the accident to be cleared, God's compassion seemed to course through me. I realized that He is always ready to rush to my aid, even when others might be inconvenienced, because He cares for me and for my specific needs.

A quiet thought echoed through my heart and mind as I sat in the traffic jam: You know, it's not always about me. Sometimes God is rushing to someone else's aid and I'm the one being inconvenienced. But during those times, the Lord is also helping me to grow in virtues like patience and compassion. Not a moment is wasted with God!

I passed Mercy Road again the other day. But I didn't even think about where it might lead, because I recognize that mercy isn't a destination. It is our Lord's ever-loving nature traveling with us along the road of life.

—Jan Peterson

Embracing God's Truth

Jan saw a beautiful illustration of God's mercy when she was caught in traffic due to a driver's mistake at the Mercy Road exit. She recognized that even when the collisions of our lives are clearly caused by our own poor choices or rebellion, God is merciful. He comes to our aid, binds up the wounded, and helps us find the right direction. When we call on Him, He is ready to respond. His mercy is available every day, regardless of the road on which we travel.

Have you ever made a mistake or poor choice that not only brought consequences for you but also negatively impacted people around you? If so, explain.

____

____

Many of what we might call mistakes or poor choices are actually disobedience and sin. Anything we do that violates the commands in God's Word is a sin. What do the following passages tell you about sin?

Romans 3:23 ________________________________

____

1 John 1:8 ________________________________

____

Whether we're comfortable admitting it or not, we all have made mistakes and we all have been disobedient or rebellious at times. What does Colossians 1:21 tell us about the impact our sins (evil behavior) have on our relationship with God?

____

____

Now read Colossians 1:22. How does this verse say we have been reconciled to God and cleansed from our sin? ____________________

____

____

Mercy is lovingly "reaching out to meet a need without considering the merit of the person who receives the aid." Read the following passages and note how each shows God's mercy.

Psalm 103:8–10 ______________________________

____

Romans 5:8–9 ______________________________

____

Romans 6:23 ______________________________

____

The greatest expression of God's merciful love is when Jesus, wearing a crown of thorns and carrying the cross on which He would be crucified, walked along what could be fittingly called Mercy Road toward Golgotha (Matthew 27:27–33). Once there, He reached out His divine arms and allowed them to be nailed to the cross. He was fully aware that we didn't deserve His aid. Yet mercy compelled Him.

In light of God's mercy toward us, we should be merciful toward others. Look at the definition of mercy listed above. When you are made aware of a need, how do you determine whether or not to help?

____

____

Ask God to help you respond as mercifully toward others as He responds to you. The love of our Lord never ends, and His mercy never fails—we can discover it afresh every day. For believers in Christ, every road on which we travel is Mercy Road.

Contributor Acknowledgments

Debbie Acklin, "Hearts Waiting"—Debbie and Perry love to travel with their children, Amy and Greg. She would enjoy hearing how God has moved in your life. E-mail her at dacklin@hotmail.com.

Sonjia Bradshaw, "Shepherding Voice"—Sonjia experienced pain and blessing in the areas of singleness and marriage, infertility and motherhood, homelessness and prosperity. As a missionary in Russia, she encountered people who have little reason for hope. Through the writing and speaking ministry Living Above Neutral, she attests that a satisfying life for both haves and have-nots comes from being close to God. For more information, visit www.SonjiaBradshaw.com.

Kathy Coleman, "An Unexpected Ministry"—Kathy is the founder of the Worldwide Mom's Day of Prayer movement. She is a Christian speaker and Bible teacher. Kathy has been married to her husband Rod for thirty-one years, and they have two grown children. Visit her Web site at www.MomsDayofPrayer.com.

Christine Callaway-Crowley, "Mother of the Groom"—Christine makes her home in Arizona, where she manages an assisted-living facility. When not working there, Christine, a board-certified biblical counselor, life-purpose coach, and life-plan facilitator, can be found writing, speaking to women's groups, teaching Bible studies, and speaking to elementary-school children about the Holocaust. Visit Christine at www.aheart4him.net.

Ruthanne Dorlon, "Avowing Trust"—Ruthanne and her husband have been married for thirty-six years. They are the parents of five adult children, three of whom are married. Ruthanne serves as the Aquatics Team Leader for RDV Sportsplex in Orlando, Florida. She is a graduate of Stetson University and a Precept Bible Study Leader.

Pam Durst, "A Beautiful Completion"—Pam still raises cattle on the Flying D Ranch, coordinates a community Bible study for women in the Texas Hill Country, and meets regularly with the Friday Girls, a support group for widows that she started after Rancher Rick died. She stays young at heart playing Star Wars with grandsons Spencer and Sean, ages six and four.

Janet Perez Eckles, "Illuminating Darkness"—Janet Perez Eckles is a conference speaker, writer, and contributing author to ten books, including the Chicken Soup for the Soul series and Guidepost books. She authored *Trials of Today, Treasures for Tomorrow: Overcoming Adversities in Life.* Visit her Web site at www.JanetPerezEckles.com.

Annette Elkins, "Hope Filled Joy"—Annette is wife to her childhood sweetheart, mother of three grown children, and grandmother to four teenagers. Continuing to live by faith, she teaches small group Bible studies to women and works in the children's ministry at her church.

Barbara Farland, "Divine Refuge"—Barbara is not only a prolific creative writer but also an accomplished business communicator. She credits her success in both arenas to the support of her husband, Terry; their quiet New Hope, Minnesota, home; and the promise of God's help. Visit her Web site at www.barbarafarland.com.

Mary Ferguson, "Beneficial Battle"—Mary is a devoted wife, mother, and grandmother. She feels compelled to encourage other women who are battling breast cancer and takes every opportunity to share her story. Mary's greatest passion is spending time making memories with family, especially her five grandchildren.

Mindy Ferguson, "Crossing Jordan" and "The Door of Hope"—Mindy Ferguson is a national speaker, Bible teacher, and the author of *Walking with God: From Slavery to Freedom* and *Living the Promised Life,* an in-depth women's Bible study. For more information or to contact Mindy, visit her Web site at www.FruitfulWord.org.

Lana Fletcher, "The Heavenly Pillowmaker"—Lana and her husband are grateful that God has strengthened their relationship through their daughter's death. Lana continues to attend a support group for parents who have lost children so that she can support other families. You may contact her at fletcher@localaccess.com.

Debbie Forrest, "A Moving Confirmation"—Debbie Forrest is a touring songwriter and worship leader. She leads worship for her local church in Houston, Texas, as well as women's retreats around the country. Feel free to visit her Web site at www.virb.com/debbieforrest or download her single "Amen," from iTunes.

Barbara Goulet, "A Heart's Longing"—Barbara is a "stay-at-home" mom who works extensively in and out of her home every day, ministering not only to her family but also to many others. Barbara is the director of women's ministries at her church, helpmate to her husband, Chris, and (of course) chief executive officer of the Goulet home. She'll have a cup of tea and a warm hug ready for you if you ever stop by.

Sister Mary Mark Graf, "Steps of Faith"—Sister Mary Mark, now age eighty-three, continues to live in a Benedictine monastery along with 110 other Benedictine Sisters. The sisters pray together three times a day. Their motto is "Pray and Work." Sister Mary Mark also works part-time in development.

Karen Granger, "Sacrificed Desire"—Karen Granger is a freelance publicist and a Christian speaker and writer. She and her husband of seven years live in South Florida and are happy to be older first-time parents of miracle baby Luke. Visit her at www.karengranger.com.

Kathryn Graves, "Grocery Money"—Kathryn and her pastor husband have been married for more than thirty years. God has continued meeting their needs in marvelous ways. To learn more about Kathryn, visit her Web site at www.kathryngraves.com.

Cyndy Gusler, "Singing over Broken Nails"—Cyndy, a wife and mom with three little ones, proclaims to be just an everyday woman longing to be used in extraordinary ways. Her deepest desire is for all women to seek God, know Him, and call Him "Abba." She currently writes and teaches Bible studies in Texas. You can contact her at cyndygusbus@gmail.com.

Tammy Harman, "Enlightening Flow"—Tammy has been married to her husband, Kurt, for twenty-eight years. They have one daughter and have privately fostered six children. In addition to her inner-city ministry, Tammy teaches women's Bible studies and junior-high Bible classes at her home church. She knows that the Lord has a strong call on her life to minister to hurting people around her and to share the peace and hope that can only come from Jesus Christ.

Amy Kidd, "The Pursuit of Today"—Amy enjoys the adventure of serving God and her four beautiful children one day at a time. She has her own business as a Kindermusik teacher and also sings on the praise team at her church and at women's events in her area. She takes every opportunity to encourage the women she meets to pursue God above anything else and to trust in Him at all times.

Karen Kilby, "Choosing Love"—Karen Kilby resides in Kingwood, Texas, with her husband, David. She is a Certified Personality Trainer with CLASServices, Inc., as well as a speaker for Stonecroft Ministries. Karen enjoys sharing her life experiences and has had several short stories published in Chicken Soup for the Soul and other publications. Please contact her at krkilby@kingwoodcable.net.

Vicky Landry, "A Message Delivered"—Vicky Landry enjoys life with her husband and two teenage children. She is a chaplain for Marketplace Chaplains and visits employees of area businesses on a weekly basis. Her passion is to introduce people to God's great heart. Her favorite venue is the Houston jails, where she ministers to women. Her pastimes include gardening and writing.

Robin Lipe, "Loving In-Laws"—Robin has a heart for women's ministry, previously serving as the coordinator of a women's Bible study for more than ten years and currently serving on the board of an organization focused on women's ministry. She has been married for more than twenty-eight years and has two sons, the older serving as a second lieutenant in the United States Army and the younger attending college.

Emma Liston, "Faithful Journey"—Emma is a devoted wife, mother, and servant of Christ. She is still walking by faith as God has commissioned her family to plant yet another church. You can contact Emma at liston30@yahoo.com.

Colleen Lohrenz, "Fruitful Overflow"—Colleen continues to trust God to fill her heart to overflowing as He provides opportunities for her to serve. She currently volunteers as an adult-education tutor and has led several women's mission trips in support of a women's ministry in a small Mexican village.

Glenda May, "Peace in the Thanksgiving"—Glenda is married to John, her best friend of thirty-two years. She is the mother of two terrific teenagers and a witness to the power of prayer. She ministers to women through small prayer groups, meeting both in her home and at her church, encouraging others to know God more intimately through prayer.

Marilyn Maynard, "Refining Delivery"—Marilyn works in higher education and is hoping to retire soon. She loves being a grandmother and looks forward to retirement so she can spend more time with her granddaughter. She and her daughter share their story so that others may know that no situation is impossible for God. You just have to let go and let Him take control.

Denise Meagher, "Moving Forward"—Since settling into their suburban home, Denise and her husband, Ted, have adopted four adorable pets. Denise also performs in community theater productions and loves sharing her passion for words on and off stage.

Tammy Nischan, "Heavenly Care"—Tammy Nischan is a middle-school teacher as well as a Christian writer and speaker. Through the death of her daughter Adrienne of SIDS and her son Nick's battle with cancer, Tammy has learned to lean on God daily and to cherish every minute of life. She lives with her husband and five children in Grayson, Kentucky. She can be reached at www.tammynischan.blogspot.com.

Lisa O'Hanahan, "Comforting Refuge"—Lisa is currently pursuing a bachelor of science degree in Spanish K-12 education, with English as a Second Language endorsement. She and her husband constantly seek to be in the will of God by continuing to serve in the ministry of Niños de Mexico. Visit their Web site at www.ninosdemexico.org.

Donna Oiland, "The Phantom Rose Exchanger"—Donna Oiland, of Radiant Joy Ministries, is a speaker and author. She lives in Lake Forest Park, Washington, with her grandson Brandon.

Barbara Parentini, "Treasured Days"—Barbara Parentini is a writer and speaker and the creator of Soaring Hearts Cards. A retired registered nurse, her life-changing story was published in *Amazing Faith*; recent contributions appear in *Daily Devotions for Writers* and *One Year Life Verse Devotional.* Visit her Web site at www.barbaraparentini.com.

Mona Parish, "Compassionate Intervention"—Mona Parish is executive director of Care Net Pregnancy Center of NW Houston. She is deeply in love with her husband, Jeff, and enjoys spending time with friends and family, including her children Layne and Justin, her son-in-law Matt, and granddog, Cindy Lou Who.

Tanya Pembleton, "Mountains Moved"—Tanya is the administrative assistant for Fruitful Word Ministries. She also is a member of the planning committee for women's ministry events at her home church, where her husband is the Group Life Minister and Administrator. Tanya and her husband live in Tomball, Texas, with their two children.

Jan Peterson, "Mercy Road" and "Sustaining Praise"—Jan lives with her family in California and is a part-time teacher. She enjoys her involvement with women's ministries through worship and as a small-group leader. Jan has a passion for writing—songwriting, stories, and scripts. You can find her songs on www.indieheaven.com. (Search: Jan Peterson)

Darlene Plumly, "Peaceful Revelation"—Darlene is the mother of a teenage son and owner of a public accounting practice. She helps others and enjoys spending time with her family and friends.

Kathy Pride, "From the Valley to the Field"—Kathy Pride is a mom, wife, friend, encourager, and writer who loves to live life passionately, with one foot over the edge. She enjoys traveling, scuba diving, and the new-to-her sport of triathlon. She lives in Pennsylvania with her husband and two daughters. She would love to hear from you at Kathy@KathyPride.com.

Carol Rhodes, "Saturday-Morning Sadness"—Carol Rhodes is a mother, grandmother, and grateful child of God. She loves people and is passionate about God's Word and shares it wherever possible, especially as teaching director of the Highland Lakes Community Bible study class.

Tina Roeder, "Compassion at Work"—Tina's duties as a wife and mother of three daughters keep her extremely busy. She is active in a variety of ministries at her church, but her passion lies with women's ministry. Her greatest joy is encouraging women to grow in their relationship with God and helping them understand how much God loves them.

Jewel Sample, "Divine Help and Heaven-Bound Kisses"—Jewel is a speaker and award-winning children's author of *Flying Hugs and Kisses* (Lifevest Publishing, Inc., 2006); Spanish-language edition *Besos y Abrazos al Aire* (Lifevest Publishing, Inc., 2006); and *Flying Hugs and Kisses Activity Book* (Lifevest Publishing, Inc., 2007). *Hallmark Magazine* (November 2007) printed Jewel's short story "Heavenly Sugar Cookies" and her favorite sugar-cookie recipe. Jewel's life goal is to inspire children to have hope and to be their very best selves through her storytelling.

Annette Sanko, "Hooligan's Hope"—Annette describes her personal walk with God as a joy. She says, "Each day, as His plan unfolds, is a gift beyond my imagination. It is my belief that we all receive blessings from the Lord each day. It is faith that brings us the vision to notice His blessed intentions."

Wendy Savino, "A Good Education"—Wendy has graduated her two homeschool students and currently cares for her elderly mother. She is known by her family as Mission Control. Her daughter is working on an English degree at the University of Texas, and her son is in the army serving as a combat medic. You can contact Wendy at wtsavino@sbcglobal.net.

Cyndi Schatzman, "Banged-Up Beauties"—Cyndi Schatzman, RN, MS, CCRN, a former nursing instructor and critical-care nurse, is an inspirational speaker and writer from Edmond, Oklahoma. She is married to her college sweetheart, Todd, and has three teenagers whom she can wrestle to the ground over candy. You can contact Cyndi at mustangok@earthlink.net.

Maribeth Spangenberg, "Sweet Generosity"—Maribeth is a wife, mother, and encourager. She writes regularly for homeschool Web sites and magazines. Her publishing credits include *Homeschool Enrichment Magazine, Eclectic Homeschool Online, Crosswalk, Praise Report, Cup of Comfort for Mothers, The Secret Place,* and *The Spirit-Led Writer.* You can see her blog at http://homeschoolenrichment.com/members/blog/maribeth/.

Paige Stewart, "Blessed Perspective"—Paige Stewart and her husband, Craig, live in Northport, Alabama, with their two boys, Ryan and Gavin. Paige works full-time as a wife and mom and is actively involved at church. She enjoys the opportunity to speak with groups and individuals about her pregnancy and time with her twin daughters.

Beth Williams, "Heavenly Minded"—Beth Williams is a singer-songwriter, worship leader, and recording artist who loves singing to, for, and about Jesus at women's retreats and other faith-based events. She and her husband are blessed to continue raising their beautiful three-year-old granddaughter, Mozelle. Learn more about Beth at her Web site: www.bethwilliamsmusic.com.

Lisa Whittle, "Friendly Reunion"—Lisa Whittle is a wife, mom, and friend with a passion for women's ministry. A sought-after communicator, Lisa has authored several books and written various articles and devotional guides. You can read more about Lisa and her ministry by going to www.lisawhittle.com.

Debbie Wong, "Orchestrated Meeting"—Debbie is living her dreams as a wife to Robert; mom to Grace, Olivia, and Joey; speaker; singer; and author. She has a solo CD, *Heart's Desire,* and she coauthored *Weddings 101* and is a contributing author to *An Expressive Heart.* Her passion is to encourage women to dream again and discover their full potential in Christ. Visit her at www.debbiewong.net.

Shelby Young, "Giving Extravagantly"—Shelby Young lives in Northern California with her husband, Neil, and their three young children, Emma, Andrew, and Joshua. Shelby is an ordinary mom who passionately seeks to see God's power and glory in her family's everyday lives.

Lucille Zimmerman, "For His Name's Sake"—Lucille Zimmerman, MA, is a counselor, writer, speaker, and teacher. She has a private counseling practice in Littleton, Colorado. She specializes in posttraumatic stress; childhood sexual abuse; and issues of shame, anxiety, low self-esteem, and depression.